Heath
BIOLOGY

TEACHER'S MASTER ASSIGNMENT GUIDE
with Ability Level Chapter Organizers

Published simultaneously in Canada
Printed in the United States of America
International Standard Book Code Number 0-669-25447-9

  3 4 5 6 7 8 9 0

D.C. Heath and Company

Lexington, Massachusetts / Toronto, Ontario

SECTION OBJECTIVES	Core	Average	Enriched	Text Section(s)	Checkpoint Item No.(s)	Chapt. Rev. Item No.(s)
NATURE OF BIOLOGY **Text Sections 1-1 to 1-7** A *Explain* the role of observation in science.	●	●	●	1-1, 1-3	1	
B *List* the eight major themes that unify the study of biology.	●	●	●	1-2	6	9, 18, 19
C *Compare* a hypothesis and a theory.	●	●	●	1-3, 1-6, 1-7	2	3, 12, 14, 23
D *Write* a hypothesis as an "If . . . then" statement.		●	●	1-3	5	14
E *Explain* how experiments are used to test hypotheses.	●	●	●	1-3, 1-4	3	4, 5, 6, 13, 15, 20, 21, 22, 23
F *List* the steps of the research method in a correct sequence.	●	●	●	1-5	4	1, 2, 7, 22
WORKING IN BIOLOGY **Text Sections 1-8 to 1-11** G *Explain* the function of tools and measurement in science.	●	●	●	1-8, 1-11	7, 9, 12	
H *Compare* and *contrast* the light microscope and the electron microscope.		●	●	1-9, 1-10	10, 11, 13	8, 10, 16
I *Describe* how the scanning electron microscope differs from the transmission electron microscope.			●	1-10	11	11,17
J *List* some of the tools used in modern biological research and *state* the function of each one.		●	●	1-11	8	

Vocabulary Review: Biology Crossword
CHAPTER I TEST

ASSESSMENT			CONTENT DEVELOPMENT/ GUIDED PRACTICE	PROCESS SKILL DEVELOPMENT/ INDEPENDENT PRACTICE
Computer Test Bank Item Numbers			Worksheets/BLM's/Transp./Readings	Laboratories
Level 1	Level 2	Level 3		
1, 31, 32	11			
2, 13	2, 33			
3, 4, 34, 35	14			
15, 36, 37	38	16		
5, 17, 18, 19, 39, 40	20, 41	42, 43, 44, 45, 46; LAB 23, 52, 53	**Enrichment: Biology Matters 1** Bioethics: What Are the Issues? **Issues in Bioethics** Case Study 1, text page 144	**Lab Activity:** A Controlled Experiment, text page 17 **Structured Lab Investigation:** 1A Laboratory Safety **Inquiry Lab Investigations:** 1B Graphing Frog Respiration 1C Designing an Experiment to Test a Hypothesis
6, 21, 51	7, 47, 48 49	22, 50	**Reteaching: Study Guide Exercise** A. Application of the Research Method **Enrichment: Study Guide Exercise** B. Critical Thinking: Solving Problems with the Research Method	**Inquiry Lab Investigation:** 1D Using the Scientific Method
8, 24, 54	55	25		**Structured Lab Investigations:** 1E Using the Microscope 1F Measuring Microscopic Objects
9, 26, 27, 56, 57	58		**Reteaching: Study Guide Exercise** C. The Compound Microscope	
59	28			
10, 29	30, 61, 62	63		

SECTION OBJECTIVES	Core	Average	Enriched	Text Section(s)	Checkpoint Item No.(s)	Chapt. Rev. Item No.(s)
BIOGENESIS: LIFE PRODUCES LIFE **Text Sections 2-1 to 2-3** A *Evaluate* the observations, hypotheses, experimental evidence, and conclusions in the spontaneous generation controversy.		●	●	2-1, 2-2, 2-3	1, 2, 3, 5, 7, 9, 10	1, 2, 3, 4, 5, 14, 15, 16, 27, 28
B *Compare* the experimental procedures used by Spallanzani with those used by Needham.	●	●	●	2-2	4, 6	13, 17, 28
C *Describe* Pasteur's contribution toward answering the question of spontaneous generation.	●	●	●	2-3	5, 8	18, 29
RECOGNIZING LIFE **Text Sections 2-4 to 2-7** D *State* the cell theory and *name* some of the scientists who developed it.	●	●	●	2-5	11, 16, 18	6, 23, 30
E *Summarize* the relationships among growth, reproduction, and inheritance.		●	●	2-6	12	20, 21
F *List* and *explain* the characteristics shared by all living things.	●	●	●	2-4, 2-5, 2-6, 2-7	13, 14, 15, 17, 18	7, 8, 9, 10, 11, 12, 19, 20, 21, 22, 24, 25, 26
Vocabulary Review: Biology Crossword **CHAPTER 2 TEST**						

ASSESSMENT			CONTENT DEVELOPMENT/ GUIDED PRACTICE	PROCESS SKILL DEVELOPMENT/ INDEPENDENT PRACTICE
Computer Test Bank Item Numbers			Worksheets/BLM's/Transp./Readings	Laboratories
Level 1	Level 2	Level 3		
1, 10, 11, 12, 41, 42	13, 43	44, 45	**Reteaching: Blackline Master** 1 Experiments Disproving Spontaneous Generation **Enrichment: Study Guide Exercise** A. Synthesis: Requirements of Micro-organisms	
2, 14, 15, 16, 46	47, 48	49		
17, 18, 19, 20	3, 21	22		**Structured Lab Investigation:** 2A Reproducing Pasteur's Experiment
4, 9, 23, 24, 25, 50, 51	26, 52	5, 58		
6, 27, 28	7, 29, 53, 54	30		
8, 31, 32, 33, 55	34, 35, 36, 56	57; LAB 37, 38, 39, 40, 59, 60	**Reteaching: Study Guide Exercise** B. Living and Nonliving Things **Enrichment:** C. Critical Thinking: Recognizing Life	**Lab Activity:** Distinguishing a Living Thing from a Nonliving Thing, text page 33

Chapter 3 Basic Chemistry

SECTION OBJECTIVES	Core	Average	Enriched	Text Section(s)	Checkpoint Item No.(s)	Chapt. Rev. Item No.(s)
COMPOSITION OF MATTER **Text Sections 3-1 to 3-4**						
A *Distinguish* among the structural features of solids, liquids, and gases.	●	●	●	3-1		1, 2, 3, 16, 17
B *List* the characteristics of electrons, protons, and neutrons.		●	●	3-2, 3-3	4	4, 5, 6, 7, 18, 27
C *Explain* the importance of chemical energy to cell processes.	●	●	●	3-3	1, 5	15, 28
D *Use* a chemical formula to state the kinds and pro-portions of atoms in a compound.		●	●	3-4	7	20
E *Distinguish* between atoms, molecules, compounds, and ions.	●	●	●	3-2, 3-4	2, 3, 6	9, 19, 26
CHANGES IN MATTER **Text Sections 3-5 to 3-9**						
F *Compare* ions, ionic bonds, and ionic substances with covalent substances and their bonds.		●	●	3-5, 3-6	8, 12, 13	10, 11, 22, 23, 24, 25
G *Identify* the components and characteristics of solutions.	●	●	●	3-8	10	12, 21, 25
H *Interpret* a chemical equation.		●	●	3-7	9	8, 28
I *Compare* the properties of polar and nonpolar solvents.			●	3-8	14	25
J *Relate* pH to the definitions of acids and bases and to the cellular environment.		●	●	3-9	11	13, 14
Vocabulary Review: Biology Crossword **CHAPTER 3 TEST**						

ASSESSMENT			CONTENT DEVELOPMENT/ GUIDED PRACTICE	PROCESS SKILL DEVELOPMENT/ INDEPENDENT PRACTICE
Computer Test Bank Item Numbers			Worksheets/BLM's/Transp./Readings	Laboratories
Level 1	Level 2	Level 3		
12, 13, 39	40	1		
3, 16, 43	44, 45	46	**Reteaching: Study Guide Exercise** A. Structure of Atoms	
17, 48	49	4		
14, 18, 41, 74	5, 42, 50, 51	15, 19		
1, 6, 11, 20, 21, 36, 37	7, 38, 52 73			
22, 23, 53 54	24, 55		**Reteaching: Study Guide Exercises** C. Covalent Bonding D. Ionic Bonding **Enrichment: Study Guide Exercise** B. Critical Thinking: Writing Chemical Formulas	
8, 25, 26, 27, 28	56			**Structured Lab Investigation:** 3A How Matter Behaves
29, 30, 57, 58	59	60, 61, 62, 63; LAB 10, 33, 34, 35, 72	**Enrichment: Study Guide Exercise** E. Synthesis: A Chemical Reaction	**Lab Activity:** Observing a Chemical Reaction, text page 47
64, 65	9, 31	32		
66, 67	68, 69, 70	71		**Structured Lab Investigation:** 3B pH of Common Substances

Chapter 4 Biomolecules

SECTION OBJECTIVES	Core	Average	Enriched	Text Section(s)	Checkpoint Item No.(s)	Chapt. Rev. Item No.(s)
CARBON AND BASIC BUILDING BLOCKS						
Text Sections 4-1 to 4-3						
A *Describe* some of the bonding properties of carbon.	●	●	●	4-1	2	2, 3, 19, 32
B *Distinguish* between families of organic compounds.		●	●	4-1, 4-2, 4-3	1	1
C *Recognize* alcohols, amines, and carboxylic acids by functional groups in organic molecules.		●	●	4-1	3, 4, 10, 12	4, 20, 28, 29
D *Summarize* the types and functions of carbohydrates.	●	●	●	4-2	5, 6, 9, 11	5, 6, 7, 8, 9, 21, 26, 27, 31, 35
E *List* the major types of lipids.	●	●	●	4-3		11, 26, 27, 34
F *Describe* the properties of lipids and their functions in cells.		●	●	4-3	7, 8, 11	10, 12, 29, 30, 33, 34
PROTEINS AND ENZYMES						
Text Sections 4-4 to 4-6						
G *Describe* the structure of an amino acid.	●	●	●	4-4	14	13, 22, 23, 28, 31
H *Diagram* the process that joins amino acids to form polypeptides and proteins.			●	4-4	15	14, 24, 31
I *Explain* how the amino acid sequence of a protein determines the shape of the protein.		●	●	4-5	16, 19	24
J *List* several functions of proteins in living things.	●	●	●	4-4	13	25
K *Discuss* how enzymes speed up chemical reactions in the cell.		●	●	4-6	17, 18, 19, 20	15, 16, 17, 18, 25, 35, 36, 37
Vocabulary Review: Biology Crossword **CHAPTER 4 TEST**						

ASSESSMENT			CONTENT DEVELOPMENT/ GUIDED PRACTICE	PROCESS SKILL DEVELOPMENT/ INDEPENDENT PRACTICE
Computer Test Bank Item Numbers			Worksheets/BLM's/Transp./Readings	Laboratories
Level 1	Level 2	Level 3		
1, 11, 39, 40	41			
12	13, 42	43		
2, 44	14, 15, 16		**Reteaching: Study Guide Exercise** A. Identifying Chemical Families	
3, 17, 45	18, 46	47	**Enrichment: Study Guide Exercise** B. Critical Thinking: Building Macro-molecules	
4, 19, 20	48	49	**Reteaching: Study Guide Exercise** C. Degree of Saturation of Fatty Acids	
5, 21, 22	50	51		
6, 52	23, 24			
7, 25	53, 54, 55		**Reteaching: Study Guide Exercise** D. Synthesis: Analyzing Macromole-cules **Blackline Master** 2 Biological Macromolecules	
26, 27, 56	8, 57	28		
29, 58, 59	9			
10, 30, 31, 32	60	33, 61, 62, 63, 64, 65 66; LAB 34, 35, 36, 37, 38		**Inquiry Lab Investigation:** 4A Enzyme Action **Lab Activity:** Properties of an Enzyme, text page 63

SECTION OBJECTIVES	Core	Average	Enriched	Text Section(s)	Checkpoint Item No.(s)	Chapt. Rev. Item No.(s)
THE CELL: THE BASIC UNIT OF LIFE						
Text Sections 5-1 to 5-6						
A *Explain* how the nucleus directs cell activity.	●	●	●	5-3	2, 8	1
B *Compare* and *contrast* animal and plant cells.	●	●	●	5-2	1, 4	25, 35
C *Discuss* the structure and functions of each organelle.	●	●	●	5-1, 5-4	3, 4, 7	8, 11–20, 21, 36, 41
D *Describe* the structure of membranes.		●	●	5-5	5	22, 32, 40
E *Identify* the layers of the cell wall.		●	●	5-6	6	22
THE CELL AND ITS ENVIRONMENT						
Text Sections 5-7 to 5-11						
F *Explain* the process of diffusion.		●	●	5-7	9, 14	2, 27, 28, 37
G *Distinguish* between permeability and selective permeability.		●	●	5-8, 5-9	10, 11	3, 4, 32, 38
H *Discuss* the movement of water by osmosis.	●	●	●	5-9	12, 15, 16	5, 26, 28, 38
I *Compare* the effects of osmosis on animal and plant cells.		●	●	5-10, 5-11	13	6, 10, 30, 31, 33, 39
THE CELL'S LIVING BOUNDARY						
Text Sections 5-12 to 5-14						
J *Define* homeostasis.	●	●	●	Introduction	22	24
K *Distinguish* between passive and active transport.		●	●	5-12	17, 19, 21	7, 23, 26, 29
L *Explain* the process of facilitated diffusion.			●	5-13	18, 21	7, 9, 29
M *Compare* and *contrast* pinocytosis and phagocytosis.			●	5-14	20	9, 29

Vocabulary Review: Biology Crossword
CHAPTER 5 TEST

ASSESSMENT			CONTENT DEVELOPMENT/ GUIDED PRACTICE	PROCESS SKILL DEVELOPMENT/ INDEPENDENT PRACTICE
Computer Test Bank Item Numbers			Worksheets/BLM's/Transp./Readings	Laboratories
Level 1	Level 2	Level 3		
36, 37, 38	10			
39, 40, 41	1, 11			
12, 13, 14, 42, 43	15, 16		**Reteaching: Blackline Master** 3 Organelles of a Typical Plant and Animal Cell **Transparency and Worksheet** 1 Organelles of a Typical Plant and Animal Cell **Review: Study Guide Exercises** A. Structure of Cells B. Plastids	**Inquiry Lab Investigation:** 5A Plant and Animal Cells
44, 45	2, 46	47	**Enrichment: Study Guide Exercise** C. Synthesis: The Plasma Membrane	
17, 18, 48	19	49		
3, 20, 21, 22	50	23, 58		
4, 24, 51	52			
53, 54	55	56, 57, 59		
25, 26, 27, 28	5	LAB 9, 34, 35, 68	**Enrichment: Study Guide Exercise** E. Critical Thinking: Another Look at Osmosis	**Lab Activity:** The Response of Plant Cells to Environmental Change, text page 86
	29, 60			
6, 30, 61	31		**Reteaching: Study Guide Exercise** D. Passive Transport	
7, 32, 62	63	64		
8, 33, 65	66	67	**Review: Study Guide Exercise** F. Active Transport	

SECTION OBJECTIVES	Core	Average	Enriched	Text Section(s)	Checkpoint Item No.(s)	Chapt. Rev. Item No.(s)
ENERGY FROM FOOD **Text Sections 6-1 to 6-5** A *Diagram* the formation and *explain* the function of ATP in a cell.	●	●	●	6-1	1, 2, 9	1, 15
B *Explain* and *locate* the fermentation process in a cell.		●	●	6-2	3, 9, 10	2, 14, 16, 26
C *Write* the general chemical equation for respiration.	●	●	●	6-3	4	5
D *Describe* and *locate* the process of aerobic respiration.		●	●	6-3, 6-4	5, 6, 7, 10, 11	4, 7, 12, 13, 16, 19, 20, 27
E *List* the conditions under which muscles operate anaerobically.	●	●	●	6-5	8, 11	3, 25, 27
PHOTOSYNTHESIS: CAPTURING THE SUN'S ENERGY **Text Sections 6-6 to 6-8** F *Write* the chemical equation for photosynthesis.	●	●	●	Introduction	12	6
G *Describe* the process of photosynthesis.		●	●	6-6, 6-7	13, 18, 19	8, 11, 20, 21, 22, 23, 24, 28, 29, 30
H *Identify* the products of the light reactions and of carbon fixation.			●	6-6, 6-7	14	
I *Locate* on a diagram where the reactions of photosynthesis occur.		●	●	6-6, 6-7	15, 16	9, 10, 21, 28
J *Compare* and *contrast* the processes of respiration and photosynthesis.	●	●	●	6-8	17	17, 18, 24

Vocabulary Review: Biology Crossword
CHAPTER 6 TEST

ASSESSMENT			CONTENT DEVELOPMENT/ GUIDED PRACTICE	PROCESS SKILL DEVELOPMENT/ INDEPENDENT PRACTICE
Computer Test Bank Item Numbers			Worksheets/BLM's/Transp./Readings	Laboratories
Level 1	Level 2	Level 3		
1, 5, 11, 12, 13	36	37	**Reteaching: Study Guide Exercise** A. ATP: The Energy Currency of the Cell	
14, 15, 38	39, 40	41	**Enrichment: Study Guide Exercise** B. Synthesis: Energy from Fermentation	**Structured Lab Investigation:** 6A Energy from Yeast Cells
2, 16, 42	3, 43	44, 56		**Inquiry Lab Investigation:** 6B Using Experimental Data to Formulate and Test a Hypothesis
4, 17, 18, 45	46		**Reteaching: Study Guide Exercise** C. Energy from Glucose **Blackline Masters** 4 Aerobic Respiration 5 Electron Transport Chain **Transparency and Worksheet** 2 Structure and Function of a Mitochondrion **Enrichment: Study Guide Exercise** D. Critical Thinking: The Citric Acid Cycle	**Inquiry Lab Investigation:** 6C How Do the Requirements of Respiration Get into Cells?
47	19, 20	48		
49, 50, 51	6, 21			
7, 22, 23, 24, 25	8	26, 52, 53, 54, 55; LAB 34, 35, 61, 62	**Reteaching: Study Guide Exercise** E. Photosynthesis	**Lab Activity:** Role of Light in Photosynthesis, text page 105
27, 63	9		**Reteaching: Blackline Masters** 6 Light Reactions of Photosynthesis 7 Calvin Cycle	
28, 29, 30	31	32		
33, 57, 58	10, 59	60		**Structured Lab Investigation:** 6D Chemistry of Combustion, Respiration, and Photosynthesis

SECTION OBJECTIVES	Core	Average	Enriched	Text Section(s)	Checkpoint Item No.(s)	Chapt. Rev. Item No.(s)
NATURE OF DNA **Text Sections 7-1 to 7-5** A *Describe* the structure of a nucleotide.	●	●	●	7-1	1	1, 7
B *Explain* the relationship between nucleotide sequence and DNA structure.		●	●	7-3	2, 6	2, 9
C *Discuss* how the structure of DNA affects a cell.	●	●	●	7-4	3	4, 18
D *Name* several key events that led to the discovery of the structure and function of DNA.	●	●	●	7-2, 7-3	5	
E *Outline* the process of DNA replication and *explain* its importance.			●	7-5	4	12, 19, 21, 23, 24
PROTEIN SYNTHESIS **Text Sections 7-6 to 7-9** F *Compare* and *contrast* DNA with RNA.	●	●	●	7-6	7	3, 5, 7, 11
G *List* the types of RNA and *explain* their functions.		●	●	7-6	8	6, 10, 14
H *Distinguish* between transcription and translation.		●	●	7-7, 7-9	9	12, 17, 19
I *Outline* the steps involved in making messenger RNA.			●	7-7	11	20
J *Describe* how a protein is made.			●	7-8, 7-9	10, 12	8, 13, 15, 16, 17, 22, 24

Vocabulary Review: Biology Crossword
CHAPTER 7 TEST

ASSESSMENT			CONTENT DEVELOPMENT/ GUIDED PRACTICE	PROCESS SKILL DEVELOPMENT/ INDEPENDENT PRACTICE
Computer Test Bank Item Numbers			Worksheets/BLM's/Transp./Readings	Laboratories
Level 1	Level 2	Level 3		
1, 11, 12, 44	13	14		
2, 15, 45	16, 46	17	**Reteaching: Transparency and Worksheet** 3 DNA Structure	**Structured Lab Investigation** 7A Isolating Nucleic Acids
3, 18, 19, 47	20	48	**Reteaching: Study Guide Exercise** B. Structure of DNA and RNA	
4, 21, 22, 49, 50		23	**Review: Study Guide Exercise** A. The Discovery of DNA	
5, 24, 51	25	52	**Reteaching: Blackline Master** 8 DNA: Structure and Replication **Transparency and Worksheet** 4 Replication	**Structured Lab Investigation:** 7B DNA Replication
6, 27, 28	58, 59	60		
7, 29, 30, 31, 61	32, 62			
8, 33, 34, 35	36, 63, 64	26, 53, 54, 55, 56, 57	**Reteaching: Blackline Master** 8A Transcription: DNA to RNA **Transparency and Worksheet** 5 Transcription: DNA to RNA **Enrichment: Study Guide Exercises** C. Synthesis: Structure of Proteins E. Critical Thinking: Transcription and Translation **Cutting Edge** Gene Silencers, text pages 120–121	**Lab Activity:** Transcription and Translation, text page 119
9, 37	38, 39, 40, 41	42		
10, 43, 65	66	67, 68, 69	**Reteaching: Study Guide Exercise** D. Mechanism of Protein Synthesis **Blackline Master** 9 Translation: RNA to Protein **Transparency and Worksheet** 6 Translation: RNA to Protein	**Structured Lab Investigation:** 7C Genetic Code

Chapter 8 Mitosis and Cell Division

SECTION OBJECTIVES	Core	Average	Enriched	Text Section(s)	Checkpoint Item No.(s)	Chapt. Rev. Item No.(s)
DIVISION OF CELLS **Text Sections 8-1 to 8-2** A *Describe* the phases of mitosis.	●	●	●	8-1	1, 5	1, 2, 3, 4, 17, 19, 25, 27
B *Identify* the role of each cell structure involved in mitosis and cell division.	●	●	●	8-1, 8-2	2, 4	1, 2, 3, 4, 7, 19, 27
C *Compare* cytokinesis in plant and animal cells.		●	●	8-2	3, 6	11, 25
SIGNIFICANCE OF MITOSIS AND CELL DIVISION **Text Sections 8-3 to 8-7** D *Explain* the importance of mitosis and cell division in unicellular and multicellular organisms.		●	●	8-3, 8-5	7	6, 9, 12
E *Explain* how surface-to-volume ratio relates to cell function.			●	8-4	8, 9	5, 8, 12, 23
F *Explain* the relationship between DNA and cell specialization.			●	8-6	10	13, 26
G *List* the levels of organization within a multicellular organism.	●	●	●	8-6	12	26
H *Describe* how mitosis and cell division aid in the replacement and regeneration of cells.		●	●	8-7	11, 13	

ASSESSMENT			CONTENT DEVELOPMENT/ GUIDED PRACTICE	PROCESS SKILL DEVELOPMENT/ INDEPENDENT PRACTICE
Computer Test Bank Item Numbers			Worksheets/BLM's/Transp./Readings	Laboratories
Level 1	Level 2	Level 3		
1, 11, 36	37, 38	39		**Structured Lab Investigation:** 8A Mitotic Cells
12, 13, 40, 41, 42	2		**Reteaching: Blackline Master** 10 Mitosis **Transparency and Worksheet** 7 Mitosis	
3, 14, 15, 43, 44	45		**Review: Study Guide Exercise** A. Cell Reproduction	
4, 16	47, 48		**Enrichment: Study Guide Exercise** C. Critical Thinking: Significance of Mitosis and Cell Division	
17	49, 50	5; LAB 23, 24, 25, 26, 58		**Lab Activity:** How the Rate of Diffusion in a Cell is Affected by the Surface-to-Volume Ratio, text page 139
6, 18, 19	20, 51	52	**Enrichment: Study Guide Exercise** B. Synthesis: Structure, Function, and Synthesis of Proteins	
21, 53, 54, 55	7		**Enrichment: Biology Matters** 2 Organ Transplants: A Second Chance at Life	
22, 56	57			

SECTION OBJECTIVES	Core	Average	Enriched	Text Section(s)	Checkpoint Item No.(s)	Chapt. Rev. Item No.(s)
REGULATION OF MITOSIS AND CELL DIVISION **Text Sections 8-8 to 8-11**						
I *State* several factors that affect the lifespan of a cell.	●	●	●	8-8	14, 18	18, 21, 22
J *List* some of the regulators that control growth in healthy cells.	●	●	●	8-9, 8-10	14, 15, 18	10, 14, 20, 21
K *List* three carcinogens and explain how each one affects the DNA.		●	●	8-11	16	15
L *Describe* how cancer cells overcome healthy cells.		●	●	8-11	17, 18	16, 24

Vocabulary Review: Biology Crossword
CHAPTER 8 TEST
Unit 1 Concept Review: Concept Mapping Exercise
Unit 1 Review, text page 145

ASSESSMENT			CONTENT DEVELOPMENT/ GUIDED PRACTICE	PROCESS SKILL DEVELOPMENT/ INDEPENDENT PRACTICE
Computer Test Bank Item Numbers			Worksheets/BLM's/Transp./Readings	Laboratories
8, 27	59, 60	61		
9, 28	62, 63			
29, 30	31, 64	32, 65, 66		
10, 33, 34, 35, 67	68	69	**Review: Study Guide Exercise** D. Growth Regulators and Cancer **Enrichment: Cutting Edge** New Weapons to Fight Cancer, text pages 140–141	

SECTION OBJECTIVES	Core	Average	Enriched	Text Section(s)	Checkpoint Item No.(s)	Chapt. Rev. Item No.(s)
PATTERNS OF INHERITANCE **Text Sections 9-1 to 9-8** A *Explain* the difference between genotype and phenotype.	●	●	●	9-4	1	4, 11, 12, 15, 17, 18, 19, 22
B *Distinguish* between a homozygous genotype and a heterozygous genotype.	●	●	●	9-4	2	12, 15, 17, 19, 20
C *State* and *give examples* for each of Mendel's principles.		●	●	9-1, 9-2, 9-3, 9-7	3	2, 3, 4, 9, 13, 14, 15, 17, 18, 19, 21, 22
D *Compare* complete dominance with codominance.		●	●	9-8	5	5, 21
E *Construct* and *interpret* Punnett squares for mono-hybrid, dihybrid crosses, and test crosses.	●	●	●	9-5, 9-6, 9-7	4	1, 19, 20
THE CELLULAR BASIS OF HEREDITY **Text Sections 9-9 to 9-12** F *Explain* what is meant by homologous chromo-somes.		●	●	9-9		8, 23
G *Distinguish* between sexual and asexual reproduc-tion.	●	●	●	9-10	6	8, 10
H *Describe* the process of meiosis.	●	●	●	9-11	7, 9	6, 7, 16, 23
I *Compare* and *contrast* mitosis and meiosis.		●	●	9-11	8	7, 16
J *Explain* how the chromosome theory accounts for the principles of segregation and independent assortment.			●	9-12	10	
Vocabulary Review: Biology Crossword **CHAPTER 9 TEST**						

ASSESSMENT			CONTENT DEVELOPMENT/ GUIDED PRACTICE	PROCESS SKILL DEVELOPMENT/ INDEPENDENT PRACTICE
Computer Test Bank Item Numbers			Worksheets/BLM's/Transp./Readings	Laboratories
Level 1	Level 2	Level 3		
1, 11, 12	33	34		
2, 13, 35	14	36		
15, 16, 37	3, 38	39, 49, LAB 5, 23, 24, 25, 50		**Inquiry Lab Investigation:** 9B Genetics—Coins and Cards **Lab Activity:** Probability and Heredity, text page 161
17, 18, 40	19, 41			
4, 20, 42, 43	44, 45, 46	21, 22, 47, 48	**Reteaching: Study Guide Exercise** C. Testcross **Review: Study Guide Exercise** A. Application of Mendelian Genetics D. Independent Assortment **Enrichment: Study Guide Exercise** B. Critical Thinking: Solving More Problems in Genetics	**Inquiry Lab Investigations:** 9A Genetics of Corn Kernels 9C Using Poker Chips to Understand Dihybrid Crosses
6, 26, 51	52, 53	54		
7, 27, 28, 29	55, 56			
8, 57, 65	30, 58		**Reteaching: Study Guide Exercise** E. Process of Meiosis **Blackline Master** 11 Meiosis **Transparency and Worksheet** 8 Meiosis	
31, 59	9, 60	61	**Enrichment: Study Guide Exercise** F. Synthesis: Comparing Mitosis and Meiosis	
10, 32, 62	63	64		

SECTION OBJECTIVES	Core	Average	Enriched	Text Section(s)	Checkpoint Item No.(s)	Chapt. Rev. Item No.(s)
CHROMOSOMES AND INHERITANCE **Text Sections 10-1 to 10-4** A *Distinguish* between autosomes and sex chromosomes.	●	●	●	10-1	1	1
B *Explain* the chromosomal basis of sex determination.		●	●	10-1	2	2, 4, 11, 18
C *Give* examples of sex-linked traits.	●	●	●	10-2, 10-3	3, 5	5, 6, 17
D *Discuss* the effect of linkage on independent assortment.		●	●	10-4	6	3, 12
E *Describe* how crossing over affects linkage.			●	10-4	4, 6	7, 12, 13, 19
CHANGES IN GENETIC MATERIAL **Text Sections 10-5 to 10-8** F *Identify* some causes of mutation.	●	●	●	10-5	7	10
G *Distinguish* between a chromosomal mutation and a gene mutation.		●	●	10-6, 10-7, 10-8	8	20
H *Give examples* of chromosomal mutations.		●	●	10-6, 10-7	9	8, 13, 16
I *Describe* the three types of gene mutations.			●	10-8	10	9, 15, 21, 22
J *Explain* how mutations are passed from one generation to another.			●	10-5, 10-8	11	14

Vocabulary Review: Biology Crossword
CHAPTER 10 TEST

ASSESSMENT			CONTENT DEVELOPMENT/ GUIDED PRACTICE	PROCESS SKILL DEVELOPMENT/ INDEPENDENT PRACTICE
Computer Test Bank Item Numbers			Worksheets/BLM's/Transp./Readings	Laboratories
Level 1	Level 2	Level 3		
1, 11, 38	39, 40	41		
2, 12, 42	13, 43	14, 44		
3, 15, 45	16, 46	17, 47, 48	**Enrichment: Study Guide Exercise** A. Synthesis: Linkage	**Structured Lab Investigations:** 10A *Drosophila* Techniques 10B *Drosophila* Crosses
4, 49, 50	18	51		
5, 19, 20, 21, 52, 53	22	54; LAB 23, 55, 56, 57	**Enrichment: Study Guide Exercise** B. Critical Thinking: Crossing Over	**Lab Activity:** Mapping Genes Using Crossover Frequency, text page 175
6, 24, 25, 58	59			
7, 26, 27	28, 60		**Review: Study Guide Exercise** C. Chromosomal Mutations	
8, 29, 30, 61	31, 62			
9, 32, 33, 34, 63	35, 64			
10, 66, 67	36	37, 65	**Enrichment: Biology Matters** 3 Genetic Screening: What to Do with a New Tool **Cutting Edge** Somatic Gene Therapy, text pages 176–177	

SECTION OBJECTIVES	Core	Average	Enriched	Text Section(s)	Checkpoint Item No.(s)	Chapt. Rev. Item No.(s)
PATTERNS OF INHERITANCE Text Sections 11-1 to 11-4						
A *Distinguish* between multiple alleles and multiple genes.	●	●	●	11-1, 11-2	1, 5, 6	1, 16
B *Give* examples of traits determined by multiple alleles and multiple genes.	●	●	●	11-1, 11-2	2	2, 3, 18, 24, 25, 27
C *Compare* sex-influenced and sex-limited inheritance.		●	●	11-3	3	4, 5, 19
D *Describe* the effect of environment on gene expression.	●	●	●	11-4	4	6
HUMAN DISORDERS Text Sections 11-5 to 11-6 E *Describe* several genetic disorders in humans.	●	●	●	11-5, 11-6	7, 9	7, 9, 10
F *State* the patterns of transmission for several genetic disorders.		●	●	11-5, 11-6	7, 8, 10, 11	8, 9, 17, 23
DETECTING DISORDERS Text Sections 11-7 to 11-9 G *Describe* several methods that are used to detect genetic disorders.			●	11-7, 11-8	14, 15	11, 12, 21, 22, 26
H *Give examples* of genetic disorders that can be detected by each method.			●	11-7, 11-8		20, 22
I *Explain* what a genetic counselor does.		●	●	11-9	12	13, 20, 21
TREATING DISORDERS Text Sections 11-10 to 11-11 J *Name* several ways in which genetic disorders are treated before birth.		●	●	11-10	16	14
K *Describe* how an inborn error of metabolism can be treated.		●	●	11-11	17, 18	15

Vocabulary Review: Biology Crossword
CHAPTER 11 TEST

ASSESSMENT			CONTENT DEVELOPMENT/ GUIDED PRACTICE	PROCESS SKILL DEVELOPMENT/ INDEPENDENT PRACTICE
Computer Test Bank Item Numbers			Worksheets/BLM's/Transp./Readings	Laboratories
Level 1	**Level 2**	**Level 3**		
11, 12, 30, 31	13, 14	15		
1, 32	33	16, 34, 35; LAB 64, 65, 66	**Reteaching: Study Guide Exercise** A. Inheritance through Multiple Alleles **Review: Study Guide Exercise** B. Inheritance through Multiple Genes	**Lab Activity:** Dihybrid Crosses, text page 195
2, 17, 18, 36, 37	38	39		**Structured Lab Investigation:** 11A Human Heredity
3, 40	41, 42	43		
4, 19, 44, 45, 46	47			
5, 6, 48, 51	20, 49, 52, 53	50, 54	**Reteaching: Study Guide Exercise** D. Disorders Caused by Nondisjunction **Enrichment: Study Guide Exercise** C. Critical Thinking: Diseases Caused by Gene Mutations	
21, 22, 55, 56	7		**Enrichment: Cutting Edge** Sequencing the Human Genome, text pages 196–197	
8, 57	23, 24, 58	59	**Enrichment: Issues in Bioethics** Case Study 1, text page 292	
25	9, 26			
10, 27, 60	61			
28, 29, 62	63		**Enrichment: Study Guide Exercise** E. Synthesis: Treating Inborn Errors of Metabolism **Issues in Bioethics** Case Study 1, text page 292	

SECTION OBJECTIVES	Core	Average	Enriched	Text Section(s)	Checkpoint Item No.(s)	Chapt. Rev. Item No.(s)
CONTROLLED BREEDING **Text Sections 12-1 to 12-3** A *Describe* the process of mass selection.	●	●	●	12-1	1	1, 2, 16, 17
B *Explain* how inbreeding is used to maintain desired traits.	●	●	●	12-2	2	3, 16, 17, 23, 24
C *Discuss* the effects of inbreeding.	●	●	●	12-2	3	4, 17, 24
D *Contrast* inbreeding and hybridization.		●	●	12-1, 12-3	4, 5, 6, 7	5, 15, 18, 19
ARTIFICIAL METHODS OF GENETIC CONTROL **Text Sections 12-4 to 12-7** E *Explain* how polyploidy in plants can be produced artificially.		●	●	12-4	8	6, 14, 15, 17
F *Describe* how plants and animals are produced by cloning.		●	●	12-5	9	7, 20, 23
G *Discuss* methods used to alter an organism's DNA.			●	12-6, 12-7	12	8, 9, 10, 21
H *Give examples* of the uses of genetic engineering.		●	●	12-6, 12-7	10	11, 12, 17
I *Discuss* some of the concerns about genetic engineering.		●	●	12-6, 12-7	11	13, 22

Vocabulary Review: Biology Crossword
CHAPTER 12 TEST

ASSESSMENT			CONTENT DEVELOPMENT/ GUIDED PRACTICE	PROCESS SKILL DEVELOPMENT/ INDEPENDENT PRACTICE
Computer Test Bank Item Numbers			Worksheets/BLM's/Transp./Readings	Laboratories
Level 1	Level 2	Level 3		
1, 10, 36, 37	11, 38	39		
2, 12, 13, 40	14, 41		**Enrichment: Study Guide Exercise** A. Critical Thinking: Problems in Applied Genetics	
3, 15, 42	16, 43			
4, 17, 18, 19, 44	45, 46		**Enrichment: Study Guide Exercise** B. Synthesis: Establishing a New Variety of Flowers	
6, 21, 22	23, 50	51		
7, 24, 52	25, 53	54, 55; LAB 5, 20, 47, 48, 49		**Structured Lab Investigation:** 12A Cloning **Lab Activity:** Production of Genetically Identical Plants by Vegetative Propagation, text page 209
8, 26, 27	28, 56	29, 57, 58	**Review: Study Guide Exercise** C. Genetic Manipulation and Control	**Structured Lab Investigation:** 12B Gene Splicing
9, 30, 31, 59	32, 33	34		
		35, 60	**Enrichment: Cutting Edge** Deliberate Release of Genetically Engineered Microbes, text pages 210–211 **Issues in Bioethics** Case Study 2, text page 144 Case Study 2, text page 440	

Chapter 13 Population Genetics

SECTION OBJECTIVES	Core	Average	Enriched	Text Section(s)	Checkpoint Item No.(s)	Chapt. Rev. Item No.(s)
VARIATION IN POPULATIONS **Text Sections 13-1 to 13-4**						
A *Describe* how organisms are grouped into species.	●	●	●	13-1	1, 7	1, 13
B *Distinguish* between a cline and a subspecies.		●	●	13-2	2, 3	3, 18
C *Explain* the concept of a gene pool.	●	●	●	13-3	4	4, 9, 12, 17
D *State* how the Hardy-Weinberg principle explains genetic equilibrium in a population.		●	●	13-4	4, 5, 8	15, 19
E *Identify* the five assumptions of the Hardy-Weinberg principle.		●	●	13-4	6	2
CHANGES IN POPULATIONS **Text Sections 13-5 to 13-9**						
F *Describe* how mutations influence genetic equilibrium.		●	●	13-5	9, 15	8, 14
G *Explain* how small population size can affect genetic equilibrium.		●	●	13-6	10	5, 10
H *Describe* how nonrandom mating and migration can affect allele frequencies.		●	●	13-7, 13-8	11, 12, 14	6, 7
I *Discuss* how interaction between genes and the environment over many generations can cause changes in allele frequencies.			●	13-9	13	11, 16, 20

Vocabulary Review: Biology Crossword
CHAPTER 13 TEST

ASSESSMENT			CONTENT DEVELOPMENT/ GUIDED PRACTICE	PROCESS SKILL DEVELOPMENT/ INDEPENDENT PRACTICE
Computer Test Bank Item Numbers			Worksheets/BLM's/Transp./Readings	Laboratories
Level 1	Level 2	Level 3		
1, 11, 35	12, 36	37		
2, 13, 38	3, 14, 39			
4, 15, 16, 17, 40, 41	18, 42	10, 34, 62, 63, 64, 65		**Lab Activity:** Understanding a Gene Pool, text page 225
5, 19, 20, 43, 44	21, 45	22, 23, 24, 25, 46	**Enrichment: Study Guide Exercise** A. Critical Thinking: Population Genetics	
6, 47, 48, 49, 66	26			**Structured Lab Investigation:** 13A Population Genetics
7, 27, 50	28	51		
29, 52	53, 54	55	**Reteaching: Study Guide Exercise** C. The Effect of Small Populations **Enrichment: Cutting Edge** Are Cheetahs on the Road to Extinction? text pages 226–227	
8, 30, 31	32, 56	57	**Enrichment: Study Guide Exercise** D. Synthesis: Migration and Gene Frequency	
9, 33, 58, 59	60	61	**Enrichment: Study Guide Exercise** B. Critical Thinking: The Effect of Harmful Genes *Biology Matters* 4 Do You Really Want to Know What Your Genes Say?	

Chapter 14 Evolution

SECTION OBJECTIVES	Core	Average	Enriched	Text Section(s)	Checkpoint Item No.(s)	Chapt. Rev. Item No.(s)
EVIDENCE OF EVOLUTION **Text Sections 14-1 to 14-5** A *Describe* how fossils form.	●	●	●	14-1	1, 3	1, 19, 20, 33
B *State* how radioactive isotopes are used to date rocks and fossils.		●	●	14-2	2, 5	2, 20, 26
C *List* and *explain* some of the supporting data for evolutionary theory.	●	●	●	14-1, 14-2, 14-3, 14-4, 14-5	4, 6, 7, 8	3, 4, 5, 6, 16, 21
THEORY OF EVOLUTION **Text Sections 14-6 to 14-7** D *Describe* Lamarck's contribution to evolutionary theory.		●	●	14-6	9, 10, 12, 13	7, 9, 17, 23, 29, 30
E *Identify* the role of variation and natural selection in Darwin's theory of evolution.	●	●	●	14-7	10, 11, 12	8, 9, 18, 23, 24, 28, 31
PROCESS OF EVOLUTION **Text Sections 14-8 to 14-13** F *Describe* the effects of natural selection on genetic equilibrium.			●	14-8	14	10, 28
G *Explain* the role of isolation in the formation of new species.		●	●	14-9	15	11, 12, 29, 32
H *Distinguish* between the processes of adaptive radiation and convergent evolution.		●	●	14-10, 14-11	17	13, 25, 27
I *Explain* how selection can stabilize a species.		●	●	14-12	16	14, 22, 25
J *Distinguish* between gradual evolution and punctuated equilibrium.	●	●	●	14-13	18	15, 25, 33

Vocabulary Review: Biology Crossword
CHAPTER 14 TEST

ASSESSMENT			CONTENT DEVELOPMENT/ GUIDED PRACTICE	PROCESS SKILL DEVELOPMENT/ INDEPENDENT PRACTICE
Computer Test Bank Item Numbers			Worksheets/BLM's/Transp./Readings	Laboratories
Level 1	Level 2	Level 3		
11, 12	1, 39	13		
2, 40, 41	42	43		
14, 15, 44, 45	16	46	**Reteaching: Study Guide Exercises** A. Evidence from Structure B. Evidence from Embryology C. Evidence from Molecular Biology	
3, 17, 47	18, 19, 20, 48			
4, 5, 21, 23, 24, 49, 50, 51	52	22, 53, 54, 55, 56; LAB 36, 37, 38		**Lab Activity:** Variations Among Individuals, text page 245
6, 7, 25, 57	26, 58		**Enrichment: Study Guide Exercise** D. Critical Thinking: Understanding Natural Selection	**Structured Lab Investigation:** 14A Natural Selection Simulation
27	28, 29, 59	30	**Reteaching: Study Guide Exercise** E. Speciation	
8, 31	61	32		
9, 33	34	62, 63	**Enrichment: Study Guide Exercise** F. Synthesis: Fitness in an Environment	
10, 35, 64	65	66		

Chapter 15 History of Life

SECTION OBJECTIVES	Core	Average	Enriched	Text Section(s)	Checkpoint Item No.(s)	Chapt. Rev. Item No.(s)
ORIGIN OF LIFE **Text Sections 15-1 to 15-3** A *Describe* the conditions on early Earth.	●	●	●	15-1	2	3, 4, 6, 22
B *State* and *give evidence* supporting the heterotroph hypothesis.		●	●	15-1	1	1, 2, 4, 5, 22, 23, 24, 31
C *Explain* the origin of the first autotrophs.		●	●	15-2	2	7, 8, 24
D *Compare* prokaryotic and eukaryotic cells.	●	●	●	15-2, 15-3	3, 4	10, 11
E *Discuss* how eukaryotic cells might have evolved from prokaryotic cells.	●	●	●	15-3	5, 6	9, 11, 12, 25, 26, 27, 32
MULTICELLULAR LIFE **Text Sections 15-4 to 15-7** F *Name* and *date* the four major eras in the history of life and briefly characterize each.	●	●	●	15-4, 15-5, 15-6, 15-7	7, 9, 10	13, 14, 16, 18, 19, 21, 30, 33
G *Describe* an explanation for the sudden appearance of multicellular organisms in the Paleozoic Era.		●	●	15-5	8, 12	16, 17, 27, 28, 33
H *Evaluate* the explanations and evidence that explain past mass extinctions.		●	●	15-5, 15-6	11	15, 20, 29
Vocabulary Review: Biology Crossword **CHAPTER 15 TEST**						

ASSESSMENT			CONTENT DEVELOPMENT/ GUIDED PRACTICE	PROCESS SKILL DEVELOPMENT/ INDEPENDENT PRACTICE
Computer Test Bank Item Numbers			Worksheets/BLM's/Transp./Readings	Laboratories
Level 1	**Level 2**	**Level 3**		
1, 2, 11, 12, 29, 30	31	LAB 7, 21, 47, 48, 49, 50	**Enrichment: Study Guide Exercise** B. Synthesis: Amino Acids Formed by the Miller Experiment	**Lab Activity:** Coacervates—A Model for Cell Evolution, text page 259
3, 13, 14, 15, 32, 33	34	35, 36		
4, 16, 37	38, 39	40	**Review: Study Guide Exercise** A. Origin of Life	
17, 41, 42	5	43		
6, 18, 44, 45, 46	19, 20			
8, 22, 23, 24, 51, 52	53, 54, 55	56	**Enrichment: Study Guide Exercise** C. Critical Thinking: Multicellular Life	**Structured Lab Investigation:** 15A Evolution of Life
25, 26	9	57		
10, 58	27, 28, 59	60		

SECTION OBJECTIVES	Core	Average	Enriched	Text Section(s)	Checkpoint Item No.(s)	Chapt. Rev. Item No.(s)
THE HUMAN AS A PRIMATE **Text Sections 16-1 to 16-2** A *Describe* the characteristics of primates and *state* how each was originally an adaptation for life in trees.	●	●	●	16-1	1, 3	1, 2, 3, 17, 25
B *List* the similarities and differences between human and ape skeletons.	●	●	●	16-2	2, 3	4, 5, 15, 25
C *State* how some of the differences between human and ape skeletons are related to bipedal walking in humans.		●	●	16-2	4, 5	6, 16, 23, 25
TRACING HUMAN EVOLUTION **Text Sections 16-3 to 16-7** D *Give* examples of evidence that reconstructs human history.	●	●	●	16-4	7	8, 14, 21, 26
E *State* why *Australopithecus* is thought to be an early human ancestor.		●	●	16-5	8	10
F *Define* the term *hominid*.	●	●	●	16-5	9	11, 20, 25
G *Identify* the characteristics that distinguish *Homo habilis*, *Homo erectus*, and *Homo sapiens*.		●	●	16-6, 16-7	11	9, 12, 18, 20, 24
H *Describe* the relationship between culture and brain evolution.					12	7, 19
I *Compare* *Homo sapiens neanderthalensis* and *Homo sapiens sapiens*.		●	●	16-7	10	13, 22
Vocabulary Review: Biology Crossword **CHAPTER 16 TEST**						

ASSESSMENT Computer Test Bank Item Numbers			CONTENT DEVELOPMENT/ GUIDED PRACTICE Worksheets/BLM's/Transp./Readings	PROCESS SKILL DEVELOPMENT/ INDEPENDENT PRACTICE Laboratories
Level 1	Level 2	Level 3		
1, 11, 12, 13, 14	15, 40	41, 42		
16, 17, 18	2, 19, 20, 21	43	**Reteaching: Study Guide Exercise** B. Apes and Humans	**Structured Lab Investigation:** 16A Comparing Indexes Among Primates
3, 22, 44	45	46		
6, 25, 49, 50	51	10, 37, 38, 39, 62, 63		**Lab Activity:** Comparing Primate Hemoglobins, text pages 272–273
7, 52, 53	54	27		
8, 28, 55	29, 56			
9, 30, 31, 32	57		**Reteaching: Study Guide Exercise** C. Comparing Hominid Fossils	
4, 23, 24, 47	5	48	**Enrichment: Study Guide Exercise** A. Synthesis: History of the Higher Primates	
33, 34, 35, 36, 58, 59	60, 61		**Enrichment: Study Guide Exercise** D. Critical Thinking: Tracing Human Evolution	

SECTION OBJECTIVES	Core	Average	Enriched	Text Section(s)	Checkpoint Item No.(s)	Chapt. Rev. Item No.(s)
SYSTEMS OF CLASSIFICATION **Text Sections 17-1 to 17-5** A *State* several reasons why systems of classification are important.	●	●	●	17-1	7	4, 18, 26
B *Explain* several advantages of using a system of binomial nomenclature.		●	●	17-1	1	2, 22, 26
C *List* the levels of classification developed by Linnaeus.	●	●	●	17-2	6	3, 13, 16, 17, 19, 20, 21
D *Describe* a modern technique used in classifying organisms.		●	●	17-3	2	7, 24
E *Explain* why two- and three-kingdom classification systems were not adequate.	●	●	●	17-4	3	1, 10, 11
F *List* the criteria used in classifying organisms within a five-kingdom system.		●	●	17-5	4, 5	6, 8, 9, 12, 15, 23
IDENTIFYING ORGANISMS **Text Sections 17-6 to 17-7** G *Explain* how organisms can be identified.	●	●	●	17-6	8, 11, 12	5, 25, 27
H *Describe* how to use a classification key.	●	●	●	17-7	9, 10, 13	14, 28, 29

Vocabulary Review: Biology Crossword
CHAPTER 17 TEST
Unit 2 Concept Review: Concept Mapping Exercise
Unit 2 Review, text page 293

ASSESSMENT Computer Test Bank Item Numbers			CONTENT DEVELOPMENT/ GUIDED PRACTICE Worksheets/BLM's/Transp./Readings	PROCESS SKILL DEVELOPMENT/ INDEPENDENT PRACTICE Laboratories
Level 1	Level 2	Level 3		
1, 11, 12, 35	13	14	**Enrichment: Cutting Edge** The Number of Species on Earth, text pages 288–289	
15, 16, 17	2, 3, 36	37		
4, 18, 19, 62	38, 39, 40	41	**Review: Study Guide Exercise** A. Primate Classification	
5, 20, 42	21, 43, 44	45, 46, 47, 48, 49		
6, 22, 23, 24, 50		51		
25, 26, 52, 53	54, 55, 56		**Enrichment: Study Guide Exercise** B. Critical Thinking: The Five-Kingdom System	
7, 27, 57	8			**Structured Lab Investigation:** 17A Constructing a Phylogenetic Tree
9, 10, 28, 29	30, 58	31; LAB 32, 33, 34, 59, 60, 61	**Enrichment: Study Guide Exercise** C. Synthesis: Using a Key to Identify Primates	**Lab Activity:** Using a Classification Key to Identify Insects, text page 287

SECTION OBJECTIVES	Core	Average	Enriched	Text Section(s)	Checkpoint Item No.(s)	Chapt. Rev. Item No.(s)
KINGDOM MONERA **Text Sections 18-1 to 18-6** A *List* the major differences between prokaryotic and eukaryotic cells.	●	●	●	18-1	1	1
B *Describe* how monerans are classified.	●	●	●	18-2, 18-3	2	2
C *Explain* how monerans obtain nutrition.		●	●	18-3	3, 4, 7	3, 4, 21
D *Identify* the ways monerans obtain energy.		●	●	18-3	5, 8	5, 14, 15, 23
E *Describe* bacterial reproduction and *explain* two ways bacteria can exchange genetic information.		●	●	18-4, 18-5	9	6
F *Discuss* the importance of monerans.	●	●	●	18-6	6	5, 7, 16
VIRUSES **Text Sections 18-7 to 18-13** G *Describe* the structure of a typical virus.	●	●	●	18-7	10	8
H *Explain* how a lytic virus replicates.		●	●	18-8	11, 14, 17	9, 18, 19, 22
I *Distinguish* between a lytic cycle and a lysogenic cycle.		●	●	18-8	12, 14, 17	10, 17, 18, 24
J *Compare* RNA viruses with DNA viruses.		●	●	18-9, 18-10, 18-11	13, 15, 18, 19	11, 18, 20
K *Explain* how viruses can cause cancer.			●	18-12	15, 20	12
L *Discuss* three explanations for the origin of viruses.			●	18-13	16	13

Vocabulary Review: Biology Crossword
CHAPTER 18 TEST

ASSESSMENT			CONTENT DEVELOPMENT/ GUIDED PRACTICE	PROCESS SKILL DEVELOPMENT/ INDEPENDENT PRACTICE
Computer Test Bank Item Numbers			Worksheets/BLM's/Transp./Readings	Laboratories
Level 1	Level 2	Level 3		
1, 11, 12	13, 41			
2, 14, 42, 43, 44	15, 16	LAB 5, 27, 28, 29, 30, 57	**Enrichment: Study Guide Exercise** A. Critical Thinking: Classification of Monerans	**Structured Lab Investigations:** 18A Bacterial Motility 18B Staining Bacteria **Lab Activity:** Growing Bacteria in the Laboratory, text page 313
17, 18, 19, 45, 73	46	47, 48, 49, 50, 51		
3, 20, 52				
21, 22	23, 53	24	**Reteaching: Study Guide Exercise** B. Reproduction of Bacteria and Recombination of Bacterial DNA **Enrichment:** *Biology Matters* 5 Genetic Engineering on the Farm	
4, 25, 54	55, 56	26		
6, 31, 58, 59, 60	61, 62	63		
7, 32, 33, 64	65			
8, 34, 35, 66			**Reteaching: Study Guide Exercise** C. Life Cycles of Viruses **Blackline Master** 12 Virus Reproduction: Lytic and Lysogenic Cycles **Transparency and Worksheet** 9 Virus Reproduction: Lytic and Lysogenic Cycles	
36, 37, 38, 67, 68, 69	9		**Enrichment: Issues in Bioethics** Case Studies 1 and 2, text page 348	
70			**Enrichment: Study Guide Exercise** D. Synthesizing: Viruses and Cancer	
10, 39	40, 71	72	**Reteaching: Study Guide Exercise** E. Are Viruses Alive?	

Chapter 19 Protists

SECTION OBJECTIVES	Core	Average	Enriched	Text Section(s)	Checkpoint Item No.(s)	Chapt. Rev. Item No.(s)
ANIMALLIKE PROTISTS **Text Sections 19-1 to 19-3** A *Explain* why the protist kingdom contains a variety of seemingly unrelated organisms.		●	●	Introduction	1	28, 35
B *List* and *describe* the functions of some of the cell organelles found in protists.		●	●	19-1, 19-2, 19-3	2, 4	1, 27
C *Name* the major groups of animallike protists and *describe* the major characteristics of each group.	●	●	●	19-1, 19-2, 19-3	3, 7, 8	1, 4, 17–26, 29, 30, 33, 35
D *Describe* reproduction in animallike protists.		●	●	19-1, 19-2, 19-3	5, 6	2, 3
PLANTLIKE PROTISTS **Text Sections 19-4 to 19-6** E *Identify* the six major groups of plantlike protists and *state* the major characteristics of each.	●	●	●	19-4, 19-5	9, 10, 13	5, 6, 7, 8, 17–26, 29, 31, 34, 35
F *Give* an example of alternation of generations in a protist.		●	●	19-5	11	11, 12, 32
G *Contrast* the life cycles found in different groups of plantlike protists.			●	19-4, 19-5, 19-6	12	9, 10, 32
FUNGUSLIKE PROTISTS **Text Sections 19-7 to 19-9** H *Name* the three major groups of funguslike protists and *state* the characteristics of each group.	●	●	●	19-7, 19-8, 19-9	14, 17, 18	13, 14, 17–26
I *Describe* the life cycle of a cellular slime mold.		●	●	19-8	15	15
J *Compare* the life cycles of acellular and cellular slime molds.			●	19-7, 19-8	16	16
Vocabulary Review: Biology Crosswords **CHAPTER 19 TEST**						

ASSESSMENT			CONTENT DEVELOPMENT/ GUIDED PRACTICE	PROCESS SKILL DEVELOPMENT/ INDEPENDENT PRACTICE
Computer Test Bank Item Numbers			Worksheets/BLM's/Transp./Readings	Laboratories
Level 1	Level 2	Level 3		
1, 11, 49, 50	51	52		
2, 12, 13, 14, 15	53, 54			
16, 17, 18, 19, 55	56, 57	20, 21, 22, 23; LAB 27, 28, 29, 60	**Reteaching: Study Guide Exercise** A. Biology of Animallike Protists **Blackline Master** 13 Conjugation of *Paramecium* **Transparency and Worksheet** 10 Structure of a Paramecium **Enrichment: Study Guide Exercise** B. Critical Thinking: Classifying Animallike Protists	**Inquiry Lab Investigation:** 19A Protists **Lab Activity:** Structure and Population Growth of *Blepharisma*, text page 333
3, 24, 58	25, 26	59	**Reteaching: Transparency and Worksheet** 11 Malaria Infection Cycle	
4, 5, 6, 7, 30, 31, 32, 61	62	33	**Reteaching: Study Guide Exercise** C. Characteristics of Plantlike Protists **Blackline Master** 14 Structure of Euglena **Transparency and Worksheet** 12 Structure of Euglena	**Structured Lab Investigation:** 19B Characteristics of Green Algae
34, 63	35, 36, 37		**Reteaching: Study Guide Exercise** D. Sexual Reproduction in Multicellular Green Algae	
8, 38, 64, 65	39, 66		**Enrichment: Study Guide Exercise** E. Synthesis: Prokaryote and Eukaryote Conjugation	
40, 41, 42, 67	43, 68	69	**Reteaching: Study Guide Exercise** F. The Funguslike Protists	
9, 44, 45	70	46		
10, 47	71, 72	48	**Reteaching: Blackline Master** 15 Life Cycle of an Acellular Slime Mold	

Chapter 20 Fungi

SECTION OBJECTIVES	Core	Average	Enriched	Text Section(s)	Checkpoint Item No.(s)	Chapt. Rev. Item No.(s)
CHARACTERISTICS OF FUNGI **Text Sections 20-1 to 20-3**						
A *Describe* the structure of a fungal hypha.	●	●	●	20-1	1, 2, 7	1, 3, 22, 24
B *List* several different ways fungi obtain food from their environment.		●	●	20-2	3, 4, 6	2, 4, 5, 18, 23, 25, 27, 35, 37
C *State* the general characteristics of fungal reproduction.	●	●	●	20-3	5, 7	3, 6, 7, 26, 38, 39, 40
VARIETY OF FUNGI **Text Sections 20-4 to 20-8**						
D *Diagram* the life cycle of a bread mold.		●	●	20-4	8, 15	8, 9, 19, 26, 28, 29, 38
E *Describe* the characteristics of fungi in the division Ascomycota.	●	●	●	20-5	9, 10	10, 20, 30, 34, 37, 38
F *Give examples* showing how specific sac fungi and club fungi affect humans.		●	●	20-5, 20-6	11	11
G *List* the characteristics that make fungi in the division Basidiomycota different from other fungi.		●	●	20-6	12, 16	12, 13, 21, 31, 32, 34, 38, 39
H *State* why some fungi are placed in a separate division.		●	●	20-7	13	14, 19, 20, 33, 41
I *Explain* why lichens are unique organisms.	●	●	●	20-8	14	15, 16, 17, 36, 41, 42

Vocabulary Review: Biology Crossword
CHAPTER 20 TEST
Unit 3 Concept Review: Concept Mapping Exercise
Unit 3 Review, text page 349

ASSESSMENT			CONTENT DEVELOPMENT/ GUIDED PRACTICE	PROCESS SKILL DEVELOPMENT/ INDEPENDENT PRACTICE
Computer Test Bank Item Numbers			Worksheets/BLM's/Transp./Readings	Laboratories
Level 1	Level 2	Level 3		
1, 11, 12, 41	42, 43			
2, 13, 14, 15, 44	45	16, 46, 47	**Enrichment: Study Guide Exercise** B. Critical Thinking: Classification and Functions of Fungi	
17, 18, 19, 48, 49	3, 20	50	**Reteaching: Study Guide Exercise** A. Characteristics of Fungi **Enrichment: Study Guide Exercise** C. Synthesis: Comparing Funguslike Protists and True Fungi	
4, 21, 22, 23	24, 25, 26	27	**Reteaching: Blackline Master** 16 Life Cycle of Rhizopus	
5, 28, 51	29, 30	31		
6, 7, 52, 53	54	55		
8, 32, 33, 34, 56	57	35	**Reteaching: Study Guide Exercise** E. Life Cycles of Fungi **Blackline Master** 17 Life Cycle of a Mushroom **Worksheet and Transparency** 13 Life Cycle of a Mushroom	
36, 58	9, 59			**Structured Lab Investigation:** 20A Studying Fungi
37, 60, 61	38, 62	LAB 10, 39, 40, 63, 64, 65	**Reteaching: Study Guide Exercise** D. Classifying Fungi	**Lab Activity:** Fungi and Lichens, text page 345

SECTION OBJECTIVES	Core	Average	Enriched	Text Section(s)	Checkpoint Item No.(s)	Chapt. Rev. Item No.(s)
ANGIOSPERMS **Text Sections 21-1 to 21-2**						
A *Give* examples of the two groups of seed plants and their uses in your daily life.	●	●	●	21-2	5, 6	25
B *List* several characteristics of angiosperms.	●	●	●	21-1	1, 2, 3	3
C *Distinguish* between monocots and dicots.		●	●	21-2	4	
FLOWERS **Text Sections 21-3 to 21-6**						
D *Name* and *state* the functions of the parts of a flower.	●	●	●	21-3	8	2, 4, 9, 15, 16, 17, 18, 19, 21, 22
E *Explain* the formation of ovules and pollen.		●	●	21-4	7, 9	5, 15
F *Relate* several adaptations of flowers to their role in pollination.		●	●	21-5	11, 12	14, 20
G *Describe* the fertilization process in angiosperms.		●	●	21-6	10	6, 7, 15
FRUITS AND DISPERSAL **Text Sections 21-7 to 21-8**						
H *Classify* various types of fruits on the basis of their structure.		●	●	21-7	13, 14, 16, 17	11, 12, 23
I *Relate* the structural characteristics of several seed types to their modes of dispersal.	●	●	●	21-8	15, 18	10, 13, 24, 26, 27

ASSESSMENT			CONTENT DEVELOPMENT/ GUIDED PRACTICE	PROCESS SKILL DEVELOPMENT/ INDEPENDENT PRACTICE
Computer Test Bank Item Numbers			Worksheets/BLM's/Transp./Readings	Laboratories
Level 1	Level 2	Level 3		
1, 11, 12	13			
2, 14, 49	50	51		
15, 16, 52	17	18	**Reteaching: Study Guide Exercise** A. Monocots and Dicots	
53, 54, 55, 56	57, 58		**Reteaching: Blackline Master** 18 Anatomy of a Flower **Review: Study Guide Exercise** B. Structure of a Flower	**Structured Lab Investigation:** 21A Flower Structure
3, 19, 20	21, 59	22	**Reteaching: Blackline Master** 18A Formation of Pollen and Eggs in a Flowering Plant **Transparency and Worksheet** 14 Formation of Pollen and Eggs in a Flowering Plant **Review: Study Guide Exercises** C. Pollen Formation D. Egg Formation	
4, 23, 24, 60	25, 61	26, 62, 63, 64	**Enrichment: Study Guide Exercise** E. Critical Thinking: Agents of Pollination	
5, 27, 28, 29, 65	66	LAB 30, 31, 32, 33	**Reteaching: Study Guide Exercise** F. Fertilization	**Lab Activity:** Germination of Pollen Grains, text page 367
34, 35	6, 36		**Reteaching: Study Guide Exercise** H. Kinds of Fruits	
37, 38	39	40	**Reteaching: Study Guide Exercise** G. Seed Dispersal	

SECTION OBJECTIVES	Core	Average	Enriched	Text Section(s)	Checkpoint Item No.(s)	Chapt. Rev. Item No.(s)
GYMNOSPERMS **Text Sections 21-9 to 21-11** J *Describe* the life cycle of a pine tree.		●	●	21-10	21, 23	8
K *Identify* several groups of gymnosperms.	●	●	●	21-9, 21-11	19	1
L *Compare* methods of reproduction of gymnosperms and angiosperms.		●	●	21-10, 21-11	20, 22	
Vocabulary Review: Biology Crossword **CHAPTER 21 TEST**						

ASSESSMENT			CONTENT DEVELOPMENT/ GUIDED PRACTICE	PROCESS SKILL DEVELOPMENT/ INDEPENDENT PRACTICE
Computer Test Bank Item Numbers			Worksheets/BLM's/Transp./Readings	Laboratories
Level 1	Level 2	Level 3		
41, 42, 43, 67	7, 8		**Reteaching: Blackline Master** 19 Life Cycle of a Conifer **Transparency and Worksheet** 15 Life Cycle of a Conifer	
44, 68	9, 45	46		
47, 48	69	10	**Enrichment: Study Guide Exercise** I. Synthesis: Gametophyte Generation in Seed Plants	

SECTION OBJECTIVES	Core	Average	Enriched	Text Section(s)	Checkpoint Item No.(s)	Chapt. Rev. Item No.(s)
DEVELOPMENT OF THE PLANT BODY Text Sections 22-1 to 22-3						
A *Label* a diagram of a monocot and dicot seed.	●	●	●	22-1	6	4
B *Explain* the importance of dormancy.		●	●	22-2	1	1, 24, 27, 30, 31
C *Name* several factors that influence germination.		●	●	22-3	5, 7	2, 26, 27, 30, 31
D *Compare* the process of germination in monocots with that in dicots.			●	22-3	2, 3, 4	3, 18, 19, 21
PLANT BODY ORGANIZATION Text Sections 22-4 to 22-5						
E *Compare* the body organization of plants and animals.	●	●	●	Introduction	8	15
F *List* and *state* the functions of the organs of seed plants.	●	●	●	22-4	12, 14	16, 20, 22, 25
G *Relate* the structures of the tissues of seed plants to their functions in the living plant.		●	●	22-5	9, 10, 11, 12, 13, 14, 15, 16	5, 6–13, 20
VEGETATIVE REPRODUCTION Text Sections 22-6 to 22-7						
H *Cite* examples of naturally occurring vegetative propagation.	●	●	●	22-6	17, 19, 21	17
I *Describe* several techniques of artificial vegetative propagation as compared to sexual reproduction.		●	●	22-7	18, 20	14, 23, 28, 29
Vocabulary Review: Biology Crossword **CHAPTER 22 TEST**						

ASSESSMENT			CONTENT DEVELOPMENT/ GUIDED PRACTICE	PROCESS SKILL DEVELOPMENT/ INDEPENDENT PRACTICE
Computer Test Bank Item Numbers			Worksheets/BLM's/Transp./Readings	Laboratories
Level 1	Level 2	Level 3		
1, 11, 12, 13, 45	14, 15		**Enrichment: Study Guide Exercise** A. Synthesis: Seed Structure in Monocots and Dicots	**Structured Lab Investigation:** 22A Seed Structure
2, 16, 46, 47	17			
3, 18, 19, 48	20, 49	50, 51, 52, 53, 54; LAB 5, 24, 25, 26, 57, 58	**Review: Study Guide Exercise** B. Seed Germination	**Structured Lab Investigation:** 22B Seed Viability **Lab Activity:** The Effect of Moisture on the Germination of Radish Seeds, text page 381
4, 21, 55, 56	22, 23		**Reteaching: Blackline Master** 20 Comparison of Monocot and Dicot Seed Structure and Germination	
6, 27, 28	29	59		
7, 30, 31, 32	33, 34, 35			
8, 60	36, 37, 38	39	**Reteaching: Study Guide Exercise** D. Organs of Seed Plants **Blackline Master** 21 Plant Tissue Types **Enrichment: Study Guide Exercise** C. Critical Thinking: Adaptations to Land	**Structured Lab Investigation:** 22C Vascular Tissues in Plants
9, 40, 41, 61	62	63	**Reteaching: Study Guide Exercise** E. Natural Vegetative Propagation	
42, 43, 64, 65	10, 44	66		

Chapter 23 Roots and Stems

SECTION OBJECTIVES	Core	Average	Enriched	Text Section(s)	Checkpoint Item No.(s)	Chapt. Rev. Item No.(s)
ROOT SYSTEMS AND GROWTH **Text Sections 23-1 to 23-5** A *State* the functions of roots.	●	●	●	23-1	1, 4, 7	1, 25, 28
B *Distinguish* between taproots and fibrous roots.	●	●	●	23-1	1	16
C *Identify* the types of cells in a longitudinal root section.		●	●	23-2	6	2, 28, 30
D *Label* and *state* the function of tissues in a cross section of a mature root.		●	●	23-3, 23-4	2, 3, 5	3, 4, 21, 22
E *Contrast* primary and secondary growth in roots.			●	23-3, 23-4	5	
F *Describe* adventitious roots.		●	●	23-5	4	17
STEM STRUCTURE AND FUNCTION **Text Sections 23-6 to 23-10** G *List* several functions of stems.	●	●	●	Introduction	8	25
H *Contrast* the structure of herbaceous monocot and dicot stems.		●	●	23-7	9	
I *Identify* the structures visible on a winter twig.	●	●	●	23-6	14	27, 29, 30
J *Name* the tissues found in a cross section of woody stem.		●	●	23-8	11	5–11, 12, 14, 21, 22, 24, 29
K *Describe* primary and secondary growth in stems.		●	●	23-9	12, 13, 14	13, 19, 24, 29
L *Give examples* of several types of modified stems.	●	●	●	23-10	10	26

ASSESSMENT			CONTENT DEVELOPMENT/ GUIDED PRACTICE	PROCESS SKILL DEVELOPMENT/ INDEPENDENT PRACTICE
Computer Test Bank Item Numbers			Worksheets/BLM's/Transp./Readings	Laboratories
Level 1	Level 2	Level 3		
1, 49	11, 50			
2, 12, 13	14			
15, 51, 52	16	17; LAB 25, 26, 56, 57, 58		**Lab Activity:** Examination of the Growing Tip of a Root, text page 399
3, 18, 19	20, 21		**Review: Study Guide Exercise** A. Structure of Roots	**Inquiry Lab Investigation:** 23A Root Cross Sections
4, 22, 53	54		**Reteaching: Blackline Master** 21A Development of Secondary Tissues in a Dicot Root **Transparency and Worksheet** 16 Development of Secondary Tissues in a Dicot Root	
23	24, 55		**Reteaching: Study Guide Exercise** B. Root Systems	
27, 28	29			
5, 30	59	31	**Reteaching: Transparency and Worksheet** 17 Cross Section of a Herbaceous Monocot and Dicot Stem	
6, 60, 61	62		**Reteaching: Study Guide Exercise** C. External Features of Stems	
7, 32, 33, 34		35	**Review: Study Guide Exercise** D. Structure of Stems	
8, 36, 75	37		**Reteaching: Blackline Master** 22 Secondary Growth in a Woody Stem **Transparency and Worksheet** 18 Secondary Growth in a Woody Stem **Enrichment: Study Guide Exercise** F. Critical Thinking: Plant Tissues	
38, 63	39, 64			

SECTION OBJECTIVES	Core	Average	Enriched	Text Section(s)	Checkpoint Item No.(s)	Chapt. Rev. Item No.(s)
CONDUCTION OF WATER AND FOOD **Text Sections 23-11 to 23-13** M *Explain* movement of water and minerals into a plant in terms of osmosis and active transport.		●	●	23-11	15	18, 23, 24, 31
N *Describe* and *relate* the structure of xylem and phloem to their functions.			●	23-12	17, 18, 21	14, 20, 22
O *State* the pressure-flow hypothesis of translocation.			●	23-13	19	15, 23, 24
P *Give an explanation* for the upward movement of water in a plant.		●	●	23-12	16, 20	23, 31
Vocabulary Review: Biology Crossword **CHAPTER 23 TEST**						

ASSESSMENT			CONTENT DEVELOPMENT/ GUIDED PRACTICE	PROCESS SKILL DEVELOPMENT/ INDEPENDENT PRACTICE
Computer Test Bank Item Numbers			Worksheets/BLM's/Transp./Readings	Laboratories
Level 1	Level 2	Level 3		
40, 65	66	67		
9, 41, 68	42			
43, 69	44	10	**Enrichment: Study Guide Exercise** E. Synthesis: Active Transport in Translocation of Food	
45, 46, 47	48	70, 71, 72, 73, 74	**Review: Study Guide Exercise** G. The Movement of Water in Plants	**Inquiry Lab Investigation:** 23B Water Transport in Plants

SECTION OBJECTIVES	Core	Average	Enriched	Text Section(s)	Checkpoint Item No.(s)	Chapt. Rev. Item No.(s)
LEAF STRUCTURE AND FUNCTION **Text Sections 24-1 to 24-7** A *Describe* the external structure of a leaf.	●	●	●	24-1, 24-3	1	8, 9, 22, 25, 34, 39
B *Identify* the structures present in a leaf cross section and *state* the function of each.		●	●	24-2, 24-4	2, 3	1, 2, 3, 4, 6, 11–15, 21, 24, 26, 27, 33
C *Relate* the structure of the stomata to the processes of gas exchange and transpiration.		●	●	24-2, 24-5, 24-6	5	3, 5, 23, 35, 36, 37
D *Discuss* the relationship of leaves to other plant parts and to the environment in transpiration.		●	●	24-5, 24-6, 24-7	4, 5, 6, 7	3, 9, 31, 32, 35, 37, 38, 40
LEAF MODIFICATIONS **Text Sections 24-8 to 24-9** E *Cite* several examples of leaf modifications.	●	●	●	24-8	8, 10, 11, 12	16–20, 28, 29, 30
F *List* several functions other than photosynthesis that leaves can perform.	●	●	●	24-8	12	7, 29, 30
G *Explain* how the adaptations of insectivorous plants allow them to grow in nutrient-poor locations.		●	●	24-9	9, 13	10
Vocabulary Review: Biology Crossword **CHAPTER 24 TEST**						

ASSESSMENT			CONTENT DEVELOPMENT/ GUIDED PRACTICE	PROCESS SKILL DEVELOPMENT/ INDEPENDENT PRACTICE
Computer Test Bank Item Numbers			Worksheets/BLM's/Transp./Readings	Laboratories
Level 1	Level 2	Level 3		
1, 11, 12, 40	41, 42, 43, 44	45	**Review: Study Guide Exercise** A. Structure of Leaves	
2, 13, 46, 47	14, 15, 16, 17	18, 48, 49	**Reteaching: Blackline Masters** 23 Variations in Leaf Structure 24 Tissue Organization of a Leaf **Transparency and Worksheet** 19 Tissue Organization of a Leaf **Review: Study Guide Exercise** B. Anatomy and Function of a Leaf **Enrichment: Study Guide Exercises** C. Synthesis: Photosynthesis D. Critical Thinking: Photosynthesis	**Inquiry Lab Investigation:** 24A Leaf Structure **Structured Lab Investigation:** 24B Chromatography of Leaf Pigments
3, 19, 20, 21, 50, 51	22	6, 26, 27, 28, 58	**Review: Study Guide Exercise** E. Function of Guard Cells	**Structured Lab Investigation:** 24C How Does CO_2 Enter a Leaf? **Lab Activity:** The Observation of Guard Cells, text page 411
4, 23, 24, 52, 53	5, 25, 54	55, 56, 57	**Enrichment:** *Biology Matters* 6 The Pros and Cons of Pesticides and Fertilizers **Issues in Bioethics** Case Study 1, text page 440	
7, 8, 29, 30	31, 32, 59	60		
9, 33, 34, 61, 62		35		
10, 36, 37, 63, 64	38	39		

Chapter 25 Plant Growth and Response

SECTION OBJECTIVES	Core	Average	Enriched	Text Section(s)	Checkpoint Item No.(s)	Chapt. Rev. Item No.(s)
PATTERNS OF PLANT GROWTH **Text Sections 25-1 to 25-4** A *Place* the stages in the life of a seed plant in the correct order.	●	●	●	25-1, 25-2	4, 5	9, 10, 18
B *Give examples* of plants with different life spans.		●	●	25-1	1, 6, 8	9, 13
C *List* four classes of plant hormones and state the function of each.		●	●	25-3	2, 7	4–8, 16, 17, 19, 22, 26
D *Explain* the cause of apical dominance.		●	●	25-4	3	11, 17, 19, 22
PLANT RESPONSE **Text Sections 25-5 to 25-8** E *Name* several types of tropisms.	●	●	●	25-5	12, 13	1, 2, 3, 12, 14, 23, 24, 25
F *Distinguish* between positive and negative tropisms.		●	●	25-5, 25-8	12	24
G *Relate* the production of auxins to plant movement.		●	●	25-5	11	3, 20, 24, 25
H *Explain* how photoperiodism causes plants to flower.			●	25-6	10, 14, 15	2, 15
I *Describe* the process of leaf senescence.			●	25-7	9	18, 21
Vocabulary Review: Biology Crossword **CHAPTER 25 TEST**						

ASSESSMENT			CONTENT DEVELOPMENT/ GUIDED PRACTICE	PROCESS SKILL DEVELOPMENT/ INDEPENDENT PRACTICE
Computer Test Bank Item Numbers			Worksheets/BLM's/Transp./Readings	Laboratories
Level 1	Level 2	Level 3		
1, 11, 38	12, 13			
2, 14, 39, 40	15, 41, 42			
3, 16, 17, 43, 44	18, 45	LAB 5, 21, 22, 50, 51, 52	**Enrichment: Study Guide Exercise** A. Critical Thinking: Plant Hormones	**Lab Activity:** The Effect of Gibberellic Acid on Stem Growth, text page 423
4, 19, 46	20, 47, 48	49	**Enrichment: Study Guide Exercise** B. Synthesis: Apical Dominance	
6, 23, 24, 53	25, 26			**Inquiry Lab Investigation:** 25A Plant Tropisms
7, 27, 28	29, 30	31		
8, 32, 54, 55	56	57, 58, 59	**Review: Study Guide Exercise** C. Plant Movements	
9, 10, 33, 60, 61, 62	63	34		
35, 36, 37	64, 65	66		

Chapter 26 Plant Diversity and Evolution

SECTION OBJECTIVES	Core	Average	Enriched	Text Section(s)	Checkpoint Item No.(s)	Chapt. Rev. Item No.(s)
PLANT KINGDOM **Text Sections 26-1 to 26-2** A *Interpret* a drawing of the plant evolutionary tree.		●	●	26-1	4, 5	3, 22, 27, 29
B *Cite* instances of the evolutionary process occurring in the plant kingdom.			●	26-1	3	1, 7, 14, 27
C *List* criteria used in plant classification.	●	●	●	26-2	1, 2	8, 30
BRYOPHYTES **Text Sections 26-3 to 26-6** D *List* several bryophyte characteristics that limit these plants to a small size and a life in moist areas.	●	●	●	26-3	6, 9, 12	4, 10, 11, 15, 28
E *Explain* the life cycle of a moss.		●	●	26-4	10	2, 6, 16, 17
F *Describe* reproduction in liverworts.		●	●	26-5	8	9, 10, 23
G *Relate* the requirements of land plants to their structures.		●	●	26-6	7, 11	26, 28, 31, 32, 33
SPORE-BEARING VASCULAR PLANTS **Text Sections 26-7 to 26-10** H *Compare* spore-bearing vascular plants to nonvascular plants and to seed plants.			●	26-7, 26-8, 26-9, 26-10	16, 17	2, 5, 18, 19, 20, 24, 29
I *Name* and *describe* several spore-bearing vascular plants that are alive today.	●	●	●	26-7, 26-8, 26-9, 26-10	13, 14	12, 13, 21, 24
J *Describe* the life cycle of a fern.		●	●	26-10	15, 16, 18	2, 6, 25

Vocabulary Review: Biology Crossword
CHAPTER 26 TEST
Unit 4 Concept Review: Concept Mapping Exercise
Unit 4 Review, text page 441

ASSESSMENT			CONTENT DEVELOPMENT/ GUIDED PRACTICE	PROCESS SKILL DEVELOPMENT/ INDEPENDENT PRACTICE
Computer Test Bank Item Numbers			Worksheets/BLM's/Transp./Readings	Laboratories
Level 1	**Level 2**	**Level 3**		
1, 30	31	32		
33	2, 11	61	**Enrichment: Study Guide Exercises** A. Critical Thinking: History of Plants C. Synthesis: The Advantage of Seed Plants	
3, 12, 34, 35, 36	37, 38	LAB 4, 13, 14, 15, 39	**Reteaching: Study Guide Exercise** B. Concept Mapping	**Lab Activity:** Characteristics that Distinguish Different Types of Plants, text page 437
5, 16, 40	41, 42	17		
6, 43	44, 45, 46	47	**Reteaching: Blackline Master** 24A Life Cycle of a Moss **Transparency and Worksheet** 20 Life Cycle of a Moss **Review: Study Guide Exercise** D. Life Cycle of Bryophytes	
7, 18, 48, 62	49			**Structured Lab Investigation:** 26A Characteristics of Bryophytes
8, 19, 50	51, 52	53, 54		
9, 55	20, 56	21	**Review: Study Guide Exercise** E. Comparison of Bryophytes and Vascular Plants **Enrichment: Study Guide Exercise** F. Synthesis: Reproduction in Vascular Plants	
10, 22, 23, 57, 58	24, 59			
25, 60	26, 27, 28	29	**Reteaching: Blackline Master** 24B Life Cycle of a Fern **Transparency and Worksheet** 21 Life Cycle of a Fern	

SECTION OBJECTIVES	Core	Average	Enriched	Text Section(s)	Checkpoint Item No.(s)	Chapt. Rev. Item No.(s)
CHARACTERISTICS OF ANIMALS **Text Sections 27-1 to 27-3**						
A *List* some of the advantages of cell specialization in multicellular animals.		●	●	27-1	1, 6	5, 13, 15, 20, 25
B *Identify* and *distinguish* the two subkingdoms of the animal kingdom.	●	●	●	27-1	2	1, 14, 25
C *Describe* the common features of development in the animal kingdom.			●	27-2	3, 4, 7	2, 3, 14, 26
D *Explain* the difference between each type of symmetry found in animals.	●	●	●	27-3	5	4, 14, 16, 27
PHYLUM PORIFERA **Text Sections 27-4 to 27-6**						
E *Identify* cells in sponges by type and function.		●	●	27-4	8, 12	6, 17, 25
F *Describe* the structure of a typical sponge.	●	●	●	27-4	9, 12, 14	8, 18, 20, 22, 23, 25
G *Explain* asexual and sexual reproduction in sponges.		●	●	27-5	10, 13	7, 19
H *Give examples* illustrating the diversity of sponges.		●	●	27-6	11	9, 23, 24
PHYLUM CNIDARIA **Text Sections 27-7 to 27-9**						
I *Compare* and *contrast* the polyp and medusa forms.			●	27-7	15	10, 22
J *Outline* the typical life cycle of a cnidarian.		●	●	27-7	16, 20	11, 19, 30
K *Describe* the body structure of the hydra.		●	●	27-8	17, 18, 19	12, 20, 21, 22, 23, 28
L *List* the major kinds of cnidarians and briefly *describe* the characteristics of each type.	●	●	●	27-9	18	12, 24, 29

Vocabulary Review: Biology Crossword
CHAPTER 27 TEST

ASSESSMENT			CONTENT DEVELOPMENT/ GUIDED PRACTICE	PROCESS SKILL DEVELOPMENT/ INDEPENDENT PRACTICE
Computer Test Bank Item Numbers			Worksheets/BLM's/Transp./Readings	Laboratories
Level 1	**Level 2**	**Level 3**		
1, 37	38, 67	39		
11, 12, 40, 41	2		**Enrichment: Study Guide Exercise** A. Synthesis: Comparison of Animallike Protists, Parazoa, and Metazoa	
3, 13, 42	43, 44	45, 46, 47	**Reteaching: Study Guide Exercise** B. Animal Development **Blackline Master** 24C Development of an Animal Embryo **Transparency and Worksheet** 22 Development of an Animal Embryo	
4, 48	49, 50	51	**Reteaching: Study Guide Exercise** C. Body Symmetry	
14	52	15		
5, 16	53, 54		**Reteaching: Study Guide Exercise** D. Structure of Sponges	
6, 17, 18	19, 55	56	**Reteaching: Blackline Master** 25 Reproduction of a Sponge **Transparency and Worksheet** 23 Reproduction of a Sponge	
20, 57	21, 58	7		
8, 22, 59	23, 60	61		
24, 25, 26	27, 28		**Reteaching: Blackline Master** 26 Life Cycle of the Jellyfish *Aurelia* **Transparency and Worksheet** 24 Life Cycle of the Jellyfish *Aurelia*	
29, 30, 62	9	31; LAB 10, 34, 35, 36, 66	**Reteaching: Blackline Master** 26A Structure of *Hydra* **Transparency and Worksheet** 25 Structure of a Hydra	**Structured Lab Investigation:** 27A Hydra **Lab Activity:** Microscopic Structure of Sponges and Cnidarians, text page 457
32, 33, 63, 64	65		**Enrichment: Study Guide Exercise** E. Critical Thinking: Comparison of Sponges and Cnidarians	

SECTION OBJECTIVES	Core	Average	Enriched	Text Section(s)	Checkpoint Item No.(s)	Chapt. Rev. Item No.(s)
PHYLUM PLATYHELMINTHES: FLATWORMS **Text Sections 28-1 to 28-4** A *Describe* the basic body structure of flatworms.	●	●	●	28-1	1	9, 10, 14
B *List* the organ systems of flatworms and *describe* the function of each system.		●	●	28-1, 28-2	2, 7	11, 19, 23, 28
C *State* how flukes differ in structure from free-living flatworms.		●	●	28-3	3, 6	2, 15, 17
D *Outline* the life cycle of a fluke.			●	28-3	4	12, 22, 24, 27
E *Explain* how tapeworms differ from other flat-worms in structure and reproduction.		●	●	28-4	5, 6	3, 15, 16, 25
PHYLUM NEMATODA: ROUNDWORMS **Text Sections 28-5 to 28-6** F *Distinguish* the body plan of roundworms from that of flatworms.	●	●	●	28-5	8, 9	2, 9, 10, 14, 18, 19, 20, 23
G *Name* and *describe* two important parasitic round-worms.	●	●	●	28-6	10, 11	4, 15, 24, 27
PHYLUM ANNELIDA: SEGMENTED WORMS **Text Sections 28-7 to 28-9** H *Compare* the structure of annelid worms with worms in other phyla.	●	●	●	28-7	12, 13	6, 9, 10, 14
I *Identify* the internal structures of the earthworm.		●	●	28-8	14, 17	1, 5, 13
J *Describe* the function of the various organ systems of the earthworm.		●	●	28-8	15, 17, 18	7, 21, 26
K *State* how leeches and polychaetes differ from earth-worms.		●	●	28-9	16	8, 15, 27

Vocabulary Review: Biology Crossword
CHAPTER 28 TEST

ASSESSMENT			CONTENT DEVELOPMENT/ GUIDED PRACTICE	PROCESS SKILL DEVELOPMENT/ INDEPENDENT PRACTICE
Computer Test Bank Item Numbers			Worksheets/BLM's/Transp./Readings	Laboratories
Level 1	Level 2	Level 3		
1, 11, 12	35, 36		**Enrichment: Study Guide Exercise** A. Synthesis: Body Shape and Gas Exchange	
2, 13, 14	37, 38	39, 40, 41	**Enrichment: Study Guide Exercise** B. Critical Thinking: Planarian Regeneration	
3, 15, 42, 43	44			
16	4, 64	17		
5, 18, 19	20, 45	46	**Reteaching: Study Guide Exercise** C. Parasitic Flatworms	
6, 21, 22, 47	48	49; LAB 7, 24, 25, 54, 55, 56		**Lab Activity:** Comparing Flatworms and Roundworms, text page 473
23, 50	51, 52	53	**Reteaching: Study Guide Exercise** D. Roundworm Parasites	
26, 57, 58, 59	8		**Reteaching: Blackline Master** 27 Cross Section of Three Types of Worms **Transparency and Worksheet** 26 Cross Section of Three Types of Worms	
27, 28, 29, 30	31, 32		**Reteaching: Blackline Master** 28 Anatomy of an Earthworm **Review: Study Guide Exercise** E. Anatomy of Three Worms	
60	33, 61	9	**Reteaching: Transparency and Worksheet** 27 Anatomy of an Earthworm **Reteaching: Study Guide Exercise** F. Earthworm Reproduction	**Structured Lab Investigation:** 28A Earthworm Dissection
10, 34, 62	63			

SECTION OBJECTIVES	Core	Average	Enriched	Text Section(s)	Checkpoint Item No.(s)	Chapt. Rev. Item No.(s)
PHYLUM MOLLUSCA **Text Sections 29-1 to 29-3** A *Explain* the significance of the trochophore larva.		●	●	29-1	1, 13	1, 14, 24, 27
B *Identify* several typical gastropods and *describe* the characteristics of the class.	●	●	●	29-1	2, 5	2, 8, 9, 10, 12, 13, 24, 25, 26
C *Describe* how bivalves differ from other mollusks.		●	●	29-2	3, 5, 6	3, 11, 15, 21, 23, 24, 26
D *Explain* how cephalopods are more highly special-ized than other mollusk classes.		●	●	29-3	4, 5, 7	5, 16, 24, 26
PHYLUM ECHINODERMATA **Text Sections 29-4 to 29-5** E *List* the major characteristics of echinoderms.	●	●	●	29-4	8, 11, 12, 13	4, 6, 17, 19, 20
F *Describe* the unique anatomical features of a starfish.		●	●	29-5	9, 10	7, 18, 22
Vocabulary Review: Biology Crossword **CHAPTER 29 TEST**						

ASSESSMENT			CONTENT DEVELOPMENT/ GUIDED PRACTICE	PROCESS SKILL DEVELOPMENT/ INDEPENDENT PRACTICE
Computer Test Bank Item Numbers			Worksheets/BLM's/Transp./Readings	Laboratories
Level 1	Level 2	Level 3		
1, 11, 12	35			
2, 3, 13, 14, 36, 37	15, 16, 38	17, 39, 40, 41		
18, 19, 20, 42, 43	44, 45	4	**Reteaching: Blackline Master** 29 Anatomy of Two Mollusks: A Garden Snail and a Clam **Transparency and Worksheet** 28 Anatomy of Two Mollusks: A Garden Snail and a Clam **Review: Study Guide Exercise** A. Structure of Mollusks **Enrichment: Study Guide Exercise** C. Synthesis: Comparing Mollusks and Annelids **Biology Matters** 7 Shellfish We Would Have Eaten	**Structured Lab Investigation:** 29A Clam Dissection
5, 21, 22, 23, 46	47, 48	6; LAB 7, 8, 24, 25, 26, 49, 50, 51, 52	**Enrichment: Study Guide Exercise** B. Critical Thinking: Structure of Cephalopods	**Lab Activity:** Structure of a Squid, text page 485
27, 28, 29, 30, 53, 54, 55	9, 56, 57	58	**Review: Study Guide Exercise** D. Classifying Mollusks and Echinoderms	
10, 31, 32, 33, 59, 60, 64	61, 62, 63	34	**Reteaching: Blackline Master** 29A Anatomy of a Starfish **Transparency and Worksheet** 29 Anatomy of a Starfish **Review: Study Guide Exercises** E. Structure and Function of the Starfish F. Comparing the Structures of a Mollusk and an Echinoderm	

SECTION OBJECTIVES	Core	Average	Enriched	Text Section(s)	Checkpoint Item No.(s)	Chapt. Rev. Item No.(s)
SUBPHYLUM CHELICERATA **Text Sections 30-1 to 30-4** A *List* the characteristics unique to arthropods.	●	●	●	30-1	1, 5	1, 2, 22, 23, 32, 33
B *Describe* the characteristics of chelicerates.		●	●	30-2	2	3, 24, 34, 35
C *Identify* the distinctive features of spiders.	●	●	●	30-3	3	4, 6, 25, 34, 35
D *Name* some chelicerates other than spiders and briefly *describe* each group.		●	●	30-4	4	5, 8
SUBPHYLUM MANDIBULATA **Text Sections 30-5 to 30-6** E *Identify* the characteristics of mandibulates and *explain* how they differ from chelicerates.		●	●	Introduction	6, 10	10, 24
F *Name* the external and internal anatomical features of the crayfish and *describe* the function of each structure.	●	●	●		7, 8	27, 34
G *Compare* and *contrast* the structure of millipedes and centipedes.		●	●	30-6	9, 11	7, 11, 27, 33
CLASS INSECTA **Text Sections 30-7 to 30-9** H *List* the basic characteristics of an insect body.	●	●	●	30-7	12, 13	9, 12, 35
I *Compare* the two types of metamorphosis observed in insects.		●	●	30-8	14, 16	13, 14, 26, 37
J *Identify* and *describe* the function of various parts of a grasshopper.	●	●	●	30-9	15, 17	15, 17, 18, 28, 36

ASSESSMENT			CONTENT DEVELOPMENT/ GUIDED PRACTICE	PROCESS SKILL DEVELOPMENT/ INDEPENDENT PRACTICE
Computer Test Bank Item Numbers			Worksheets/BLM's/Transp./Readings	Laboratories
Level 1	**Level 2**	**Level 3**		
11, 40	41	42		
1, 12, 13	43			
2, 14, 15	44, 45		**Reteaching: Study Guide Exercise** A. Arachnids **Blackline Master** 29B Anatomy of a Female Spider **Transparency and Worksheet** 30 Anatomy of a Female Spider	
3, 46	4, 47			
48	5, 49	50		
16, 17, 18	19, 20		**Reteaching: Study Guide Exercise** B. Crustaceans **Blackline Master** 29C Anatomy of a Crayfish **Transparency and Worksheet** 31 Anatomy of a Crayfish	**Structured Lab Investigation:** 30A Crayfish Dissection
6, 51, 52	53			
7, 21, 54	22, 55	56, 57; LAB 37, 38, 39, 66		**Lab Activity:** Observing Insect Behavior, text page 505
23, 24	25, 58	26		
8, 27, 59, 60	61		**Reteaching: Study Guide Exercise** C. Anatomy of a Grasshopper **Transparency and Worksheet** 32 Anatomy of a Grasshopper **Enrichment: Study Guide Exercise** D. Synthesis: Circulation and Respiration	**Structured Lab Investigation:** 30B Grasshopper Dissection

SECTION OBJECTIVES	Core	Average	Enriched	Text Section(s)	Checkpoint Item No.(s)	Chapt. Rev. Item No.(s)
DIVERSITY OF INSECTS **Text Sections 30-10 to 30-13** K *Describe* some of the specific feeding adaptations of insects.		●	●	30-10	18	29
L *List* some of the ways color and shape adapt various insects to their environment.	●	●	●	30-11	19, 22, 23	19, 30
M *Identify* some specific reproductive adaptations in insects.		●	●	30-12	20	16, 20
N *Explain* how social insects differ from nonsocial species.		●	●	30-13	21	21, 31
Vocabulary Review: Biology Crossword **CHAPTER 30 TEST** **Unit 5 Concept Review:** Concept Mapping Exercise **Unit 5 Review,** text page 509						

ASSESSMENT Computer Test Bank Item Numbers			CONTENT DEVELOPMENT/ GUIDED PRACTICE Worksheets/BLM's/Transp./Readings	PROCESS SKILL DEVELOPMENT/ INDEPENDENT PRACTICE Laboratories
Level 1	Level 2	Level 3		
28, 29, 62	63			
9, 30	31	32		
10, 33, 34		35		
36, 64		65	**Enrichment: Study Guide Exercise** E. Critical Thinking: Social Insects	

Chapter 31 Vertebrates

SECTION OBJECTIVES	Core	Average	Enriched	Text Section(s)	Checkpoint Item No.(s)	Chapt. Rev. Item No.(s)
PHYLUM CHORDATA **Text Sections 31-1 to 31-2**						
A *List* the three characteristics common to all chordates.		●	●	31-1	1, 3, 4	1, 2, 3, 22, 23, 25, 28, 29, 30, 31
B *Name* and *describe* the three subphyla of chordates.		●	●	31-2	2, 4	3, 4, 12, 13, 14, 21, 24, 25, 26, 28, 29
VERTEBRATES **Text Sections 31-3 to 31-6** C *Identify* the major characteristics of vertebrates.	●	●	●	31-3	5	5, 6, 8, 15, 17, 20, 25, 27, 30, 31
D *Name* and *describe* the major classes of vertebrates.	●	●	●	31-4	6, 8	7, 9, 18, 19, 23
E *List* the major trends in the evolution of the vertebrates.			●	31-5, 31-6	7, 8, 9	10, 16, 27, 31
Vocabulary Review: Biology Crossword **CHAPTER 31 TEST**						

ASSESSMENT			CONTENT DEVELOPMENT/ GUIDED PRACTICE	PROCESS SKILL DEVELOPMENT/ INDEPENDENT PRACTICE
Computer Test Bank Item Numbers			Worksheets/BLM's/Transp./Readings	Laboratories
Level 1	Level 2	Level 3		
1, 11, 12, 13, 14, 15, 40	2, 41	16		
3, 4, 17, 18, 19, 20, 42	43, 44	LAB 5, 21, 22, 23, 24, 25, 26, 27, 28, 45	**Reteaching: Study Guide Exercises** A. Characteristics of Chordates C. Concept Mapping	**Lab Activity:** Structure of a Primitive Chordate, text page 521
29, 30, 46, 47, 48	6, 49, 50	7, 51	**Enrichment: Study Guide Exercise** B. Synthesis: Comparing Vertebrates with Annelids and Arthropods	
8, 31, 32, 33, 34, 52, 53	35, 36, 54	55, 56, 57	**Reteaching: Study Guide Exercise** E. Classification of Chordates	**Structured Lab Investigation:** 31A Homologies in Vertebrate Skeletons
9, 37, 38, 58, 59, 60	10, 39, 61	62	**Enrichment: Study Guide Exercise** D. Critical Thinking: Evolutionary Trends in Vertebrates	

SECTION OBJECTIVES	Core	Average	Enriched	Text Section(s)	Checkpoint Item No.(s)	Chapt. Rev. Item No.(s)
JAWLESS FISH **Text Section 32-1** A *Identify* and *describe* the two types of jawless fish.		●	●	32-1	1, 3	1, 22
B *List* the principal characteristics of the jawless fish.	●	●	●	32-1	2, 4	2, 3, 18, 21, 22, 24
CARTILAGE FISH **Text Sections 32-2 to 32-7** C *Compare* the skeleton of a shark to the skeleton of other vertebrates.		●	●	32-2	5	4, 17, 19, 22, 23
D *Describe* the unique features of skin and teeth in sharks.	●	●	●	32-3	10	5
E *Explain* how sharks exchange gases with the environment.		●	●	32-4	7	6, 25
F *State* how sharks regulate their body temperature.		●	●	32-5	8	7
G *Identify* the unusual features of shark reproduction.		●	●	32-6	9	8
H *Name* other members of the Chondrichthyes.		●	●	32-7	6	9, 26, 36
BONY FISH **Text Sections 32-8 to 32-14** I *Compare* the external anatomy of bony fish to that of the shark.	●	●	●	32-8	11, 20	10, 23, 27
J *Identify* the organs of digestion and excretion in bony fish.		●	●	32-9	12	11, 28
K *Trace* the path of circulation in bony fish and show where gas exchange occurs.		●	●	32-10	13, 14	12, 25, 29, 35, 37
L *Describe* the nervous system and senses of bony fish.		●	●	32-11	15	13, 31, 38

ASSESSMENT			CONTENT DEVELOPMENT/ GUIDED PRACTICE	PROCESS SKILL DEVELOPMENT/ INDEPENDENT PRACTICE
Computer Test Bank Item Numbers			Worksheets/BLM's/Transp./Readings	Laboratories
Level 1	Level 2	Level 3		
1	11, 35	36		
2,12	37		**Reteaching: Study Guide Exercise** A. Lampreys	
3, 38	39			
4, 13	40	41		
14	15	42	**Reteaching: Study Guide Exercise** B. Sharks	
5, 16				
6, 17	43			
7, 44	18, 45			
8, 46	47		**Reteaching: Study Guide Exercise** C. External Anatomy of a Bony Fish	
9, 19	20, 21		**Review: Study Guide Exercise** D. Digestion and Excretion in Fish	
22, 23, 48	49, 60	50, 51; LAB 31, 32, 33, 34	**Reteaching: Study Guide Exercise** G. Comparison of Three Classes of Fish **Review: Study Guide Exercise** E. Synthesis: Two Kinds of Gills **Enrichment: Study Guide Exercise** F. Critical Thinking: Gas Exchange in Fish	**Inquiry Lab Investigation:** 32B Creating a Standard Curve **Lab Activity:** The Respiratory Rate of a Goldfish, text page 537
24, 25, 52	53	10	**Reteaching: Blackline Master** 30 Anatomy of a Perch **Transparency and Worksheet** 33 Anatomy of a Perch **Review: Study Guide Exercises** H. The Brain of a Perch I. Internal Anatomy of a Bony Fish	**Structured Lab Investigation:** 32A Perch Dissection

SECTION OBJECTIVES	Core	Average	Enriched	Text Section(s)	Checkpoint Item No.(s)	Chapt. Rev. Item No.(s)
M *Compare* reproduction in bony fish with reproduction in sharks.			●	32-12	19	14, 32
N *List* some adaptations of bony fish.		●	●	32-13	17, 18	15, 20, 28, 30, 33, 34, 36, 39, 40
O *Name* the group of fish thought to be ancestors of terrestrial animals and *describe* their features		●	●	32-14	16	16
Vocabulary Review: Biology Crossword **CHAPTER 32 TEST**						

ASSESSMENT			CONTENT DEVELOPMENT/ GUIDED PRACTICE	PROCESS SKILL DEVELOPMENT/ INDEPENDENT PRACTICE
Computer Test Bank Item Numbers			Worksheets/BLM's/Transp./Readings	Laboratories
Level 1	Level 2	Level 3		
26, 27	54			
28, 55	56	57	**Enrichment:** *Biology Matters* 8 Fishing Grounds, Drilling Grounds	
29, 30, 58	59			

SECTION OBJECTIVES	Core	Average	Enriched	Text Section(s)	Checkpoint Item No.(s)	Chapt. Rev. Item No.(s)
CHARACTERISTICS OF AMPHIBIANS **Text Sections 33-1 to 33-9** A *List* the basic characteristics of amphibians.	●	●	●	33-1	8	7, 22
B *Identify* important external structures and adaptations of the frog.	●	●	●	33-2	1	10, 17
C *Compare* and *contrast* the frog and the fish skeleton.		●	●	33-3	2	5, 26
D *Identify* and *explain* the function of the digestive and excretory organs of the frog.		●	●	33-4	3	1, 23
E *Describe* the structure and function of the frog's circulatory system.		●	●	33-5	4	12, 16, 24
F *Describe* the structure of the frog's respiratory system.		●	●	33-6	5	9, 13, 19, 21, 25
G *Identify* important parts of the frog's nervous system.		●	●	33-7	6	11, 14, 27
H *List* some of the sensory adaptations of the frog.		●	●	33-8	7	2, 14
I *Describe* reproduction and development in frogs.		●	●	33-9	8, 9	4, 15, 28

ASSESSMENT			CONTENT DEVELOPMENT/ GUIDED PRACTICE	PROCESS SKILL DEVELOPMENT/ INDEPENDENT PRACTICE
Computer Test Bank Item Numbers			Worksheets/BLM's/Transp./Readings	Laboratories
Level 1	Level 2	Level 3		
1, 11	12	33		
2, 13, 14, 15		34		
3, 16, 35	36			
4, 17, 18, 37	19, 20	38, 39, 40	**Reteaching: Study Guide Exercise** A. Digestion in a Frog **Blackline Master** 30A Digestive System of a Frog **Transparency and Worksheet** 35 Digestive System of a Frog	
21, 41, 42	43, 44		**Reteaching: Study Guide Exercise** B. Excretion and Circulation in a Frog **Blackline Master** 30B Circulatory and Excretory Systems of a Frog **Transparency and Worksheet** 36 Circulatory and Excretory Systems of a Frog **Enrichment: Study Guide Exercise** C. Critical Thinking: Comparing Circulatory Systems	
5, 22	45	23		
6, 24, 46	47	48	**Reteaching: Blackline Master** 30C Nervous and Muscular Systems of a Frog	
7, 25	49, 50		**Reteaching: Transparency and Worksheet** 34 Nervous and Muscular Systems of a Frog	
8, 26, 27, 51	52	LAB 9, 28, 29, 53, 62	**Reteaching: Blackline Master** 30D Reproductive Systems of a Male and a Female Frog **Transparency and Worksheet** 37 Reproductive Systems of a Male and a Female Frog	**Structured Lab Investigation:** 33A Frog Dissection **Lab Activity:** Frog Development, text page 553

SECTION OBJECTIVES	Core	Average	Enriched	Text Section(s)	Checkpoint Item No.(s)	Chapt. Rev. Item No.(s)
OTHER AMPHIBIANS **Text Sections 33-10 to 33-12** J *Compare* the structure of urodeles and anurans.			●	33-10	10, 12	8
K *Describe* the unique features of Apoda.			●	33-11	13, 15	3, 20
L *Explain* the significance of the amphibian fossil record.			●	33-12	11, 14	6, 18, 22, 26
Vocabulary Review: Biology Crossword **CHAPTER 33 TEST**						

ASSESSMENT			CONTENT DEVELOPMENT/ GUIDED PRACTICE	PROCESS SKILL DEVELOPMENT/ INDEPENDENT PRACTICE
Computer Test Bank Item Numbers			Worksheets/BLM's/Transp./Readings	Laboratories
Level 1	Level 2	Level 3		
10, 30, 54	55			
56	57, 58	59	**Reteaching: Study Guide Exercise** D. Comparing Amphibians	
31, 60	61	32	**Enrichment: Study Guide Exercise** E. Synthesis: Comparing Amphibians and Fish	

SECTION OBJECTIVES	Core	Average	Enriched	Text Section(s)	Checkpoint Item No.(s)	Chapt. Rev. Item No.(s)
CHARACTERISTICS OF REPTILES **Text Sections 34-1 to 34-2** A *Compare* and *contrast* the characteristics of reptiles to those of amphibians.	●	●	●	34-1	1, 3	1, 4, 11, 24, 29, 32, 35
B *Name* the various parts of a reptile egg and explain the function of each part.			●	34-2	2, 4	2, 3, 35
MODERN REPTILES **Text Sections 34-3 to 34-8** C *Describe* the important anatomical features of snakes.	●	●	●	34-3	5, 6	5, 6, 11, 18, 19, 25, 32, 36
D *List* some adaptations of different snakes.		●	●	34-4	7	7, 19, 26, 31, 36
E *Compare* lizards with snakes.	●	●	●	34-5	8	8, 20, 27, 30
F *State* some of the unique features of turtles.		●	●	34-6	10	9, 28
G *Compare* and *contrast* alligators and crocodiles.		●	●	34-7	11	10, 17, 21
H *Explain* why the tuatara is considered a primitive reptile.			●	34-8	9	12, 13, 22, 37
REPTILE EVOLUTION **Text Sections 34-9 to 34-10** I *Identify* the two major dinosaur groups.	●	●	●	34-9	12, 14	14
J *List* and *describe* other types of extinct reptiles.		●	●	34-10	13, 14, 15	15, 16, 23, 33
Vocabulary Review: Biology Crossword **CHAPTER 34 TEST**						

ASSESSMENT			CONTENT DEVELOPMENT/ GUIDED PRACTICE	PROCESS SKILL DEVELOPMENT/ INDEPENDENT PRACTICE
Computer Test Bank Item Numbers			Worksheets/BLM's/Transp./Readings	Laboratories
Level 1	Level 2	Level 3		
1, 11, 41	42	12, 43, 44, 45		
13, 14, 15, 16	17		**Enrichment: Study Guide Exercise** B. Critical Thinking: Reptile Eggs	
2, 18, 19	20, 21	22	**Enrichment: Study Guide Exercise** A. Synthesis: Comparison of a Reptile and an Amphibian	
3, 23, 24, 46	47		**Review: Study Guide Exercise** C. Poisonous Snakes	
4, 25	48, 49	50; LAB 8, 32, 33, 34, 35, 38	**Reteaching: Study Guide Exercise** E. Concept Mapping	**Lab Activity:** Color Change in a Chameleon, text page 567
5, 26, 27	51, 52			**Inquiry Lab Investigation:** 34A Reptilian Adaptations to Land
6, 28, 29, 53	54, 55			
30, 56	7, 31	57	**Reteaching: Study Guide Exercise** D. Four Orders of Reptiles	
9, 36, 37	38, 59	60		
10, 39, 61, 64	40, 62, 63			

Chapter 35   Birds

SECTION OBJECTIVES	Core	Average	Enriched	Text Section(s)	Checkpoint Item No.(s)	Chapt. Rev. Item No.(s)
CHARACTERISTICS OF BIRDS **Text Sections 35-1 to 35-4**						
A *Compare* the features of *Protoavis* with those of birds and reptiles.		●	●	35-1	1	4, 8, 18, 30
B *Describe* three types of feathers and explain how each one functions.		●	●	35-2	3, 6	9, 12a–c, 22, 27, 29
C *List* and *explain* the function of the external features of a bird.	●	●	●	35-3, 35-4	5, 7	1, 2, 3, 16, 27
D *Discuss* ways in which the structure of the feet and wings reflect a bird's way of life.				35-4	2, 4	13
INTERNAL FEATURES OF BIRDS **Text Sections 35-5 to 35-12**						
E *Explain* how a bird's skeleton is adapted for flight.		●	●	35-5	8	5, 12e, 19
F *Relate* the energy requirements of a bird to the function of each of its body systems.		●	●	35-6	10, 13	12d, 12f, 20, 23, 31
G *Describe* how the internal organs of a bird are adapted for flight.		●	●	35-6, 35-7, 35-8, 35-9, 35-10, 35-11	9	6, 12f, 19, 24, 25, 26
H *Cite* examples of complex behavior in birds.			●	35-11	11	21, 32
I *Discuss* reproduction and development in birds.		●	●	35-11, 35-12	12	7, 10, 11, 12g, 14, 15, 17, 21, 28, 32

Vocabulary Review: Biology Crossword
CHAPTER 35 TEST

ASSESSMENT			CONTENT DEVELOPMENT/ GUIDED PRACTICE	PROCESS SKILL DEVELOPMENT/ INDEPENDENT PRACTICE
Computer Test Bank Item Numbers			Worksheets/BLM's/Transp./Readings	Laboratories
Level 1	Level 2	Level 3		
1, 2, 11	42			
3, 4, 12, 13, 43	14, 15, 44		**Review: Study Guide Exercise** A. Feathers	
16, 17, 18, 45	5, 46	19		
47	48, 49	50	**Enrichment: Study Guide Exercise** B. Critical Thinking: Bird Adaptations	**Structured Lab Investigation:** 35A Adaptations of Birds
20, 21, 22	51	52; LAB 39, 40, 41, 64	**Reteaching: Blackline Master** 31 Skeleton of a Typical Bird **Review: Study Guide Exercise** C. The Skeleton of Birds	**Lab Activity:** Density of Bones, text page 583
6, 7, 23, 24, 53	54		**Enrichment: Study Guide Exercise** D. Synthesis: Comparison of Animal Digestive Tracts	
25, 26, 27, 55	28, 29	8	**Reteaching: Blackline Master** 32 Internal Anatomy of a Typical Bird **Transparency and Worksheet** 38 Internal Anatomy of a Typical Bird	
9, 30, 56	31, 57	58		
10, 32, 33, 34, 59	35, 36, 37	38, 60, 61, 62, 63		

SECTION OBJECTIVES	Core	Average	Enriched	Text Section(s)	Checkpoint Item No.(s)	Chapt. Rev. Item No.(s)
CHARACTERISTICS OF MAMMALS						
Text Sections 36-1 to 36-2						
A *List* and *describe* the structural characteristics of mammals.	●	●	●	36-1	1	1, 20, 27
B *Describe* the mammalian circulatory system.		●	●	36-1	2	20, 25
C *Explain* the function of each of the four skin glands.		●	●	36-1	3	15, 20
D *Discuss* the development of mammalian young.		●	●	36-2	4	22, 28
MONOTREMES AND MARSUPIALS						
Text Sections 36-3 to 36-5						
E *Discuss* the geographic distribution of marsupials and monotremes.		●	●	36-3, 36-5	6	6, 30
F *Identify* and *describe* the three species of monotremes.		●	●	36-3	5	5
G *List* the characteristics of monotremes.	●	●	●	36-3	7, 10	21
H *Describe* the characteristics of marsupials.	●	●	●	36-4, 36-5	8	21
I *Explain* the developmental process in marsupials.		●	●	36-4, 36-5	9, 10	3, 17
PLACENTAL MAMMALS						
Text Sections 36-6 to 36-7						
J *Explain* how young placental mammals differ from monotremes and marsupials.		●	●	Introduction	17	21
K *List* the characteristics of placental mammals.	●	●	●	36-6	11	17, 21
L *Discuss* the function of the placenta.		●	●	36-6	12, 15	26
M *Name* and *describe* some of the major orders of placental mammals.		●	●	36-7	13, 14, 16	2, 7–12, 16, 18, 19, 23, 29

ASSESSMENT			CONTENT DEVELOPMENT/ GUIDED PRACTICE	PROCESS SKILL DEVELOPMENT/ INDEPENDENT PRACTICE
Computer Test Bank Item Numbers			Worksheets/BLM's/Transp./Readings	Laboratories
Level 1	Level 2	Level 3		
1, 11, 12, 13, 38		LAB 35, 36, 37		**Lab Activity:** Effect of Temperature on Respiration, text page 601
2	39	40		
3, 41	14	42, 43, 44		
4, 15	45	16	**Enrichment: Study Guide Exercise** A. Synthesis: Mammals and Other Vertebrates	
17, 18	19			
5, 46, 47	20			
21, 22, 48	49			
23, 50	6, 51			
7, 24	25	26		
27, 28, 52	53			
8, 54	29	30	**Review: Study Guide Exercise** B. Comparing the Three Subclasses of Mammals	**Structured Lab Investigation:** 36A Fetal Pig Dissection
31, 32, 55	56			
57	58, 59	33	**Reteaching: Study Guide Exercise** C. Diversity of Mammals **Enrichment: Study Guide Exercise** D. Critical Thinking: Primates	

SECTION OBJECTIVES	Core	Average	Enriched	Text Section(s)	Checkpoint Item No.(s)	Chapt. Rev. Item No.(s)
MAMMAL EVOLUTION **Text Sections 36-8 to 36-9** N *Summarize* the events that gave rise to mammals.			●	36-8	18	4, 24, 31
O *Describe* the appearance of early mammals.			●	36-9	19, 21	13
P *Compare* the modern horse, *Equus,* to its primitive ancestor, *Hyracotherium.*			●	36-9	20, 22	14
Vocabulary Review: Biology Crossword **CHAPTER 36 TEST** **Unit 6 Concept Review:** Concept Mapping Exercise **Unit 6 Review,** text page 611						

ASSESSMENT			CONTENT DEVELOPMENT/ GUIDED PRACTICE	PROCESS SKILL DEVELOPMENT/ INDEPENDENT PRACTICE
Computer Test Bank Item Numbers			Worksheets/BLM's/Transp./Readings	Laboratories
Level 1	Level 2	Level 3		
9	60	34		
10, 61	62, 63			
64	65, 66			

SECTION OBJECTIVES	Core	Average	Enriched	Text Section(s)	Checkpoint Item No.(s)	Chapt. Rev. Item No.(s)
HUMAN SKELETON **Text Sections 37-1 to 37-2** A *Name* the four basic types of tissue that make up the human body.	●	●	●	Introduction, 37-1	1	1, 2, 15, 24
B *Compare* and *contrast* the structure and function of cartilage and bone.	●	●	●	37-1	2, 4	4, 5, 14, 29, 33
C *Identify* the different types of joints in the body and *describe* the range in each type.		●	●	37-2	3, 4	3, 6, 18, 24, 30
MUSCLES AND SKIN **Text Sections 37-3 to 37-7** D *Describe* the structures of striated muscle.		●	●	37-3	5	9, 16, 19
E *Explain* the mechanism of contraction in skeletal muscle.		●	●	37-4	6	10, 16
F *Identify* the energy source for muscle contraction.		●	●	37-4	8, 12	8, 13, 17, 25
G *State* how antagonist muscle pairs function.	●	●	●	37-5	7, 11	12, 21, 24, 26, 31
H *Compare* and *contrast* smooth muscle, cardiac muscle, and striated muscle.		●	●	37-3, 37-6	9	11, 17, 22, 27
I *Describe* the structure and function of human skin.	●	●	●	37-7	10	7, 15, 23, 28, 32
Vocabulary Review: Biology Crossword **CHAPTER 37 TEST**						

ASSESSMENT			CONTENT DEVELOPMENT/ GUIDED PRACTICE	PROCESS SKILL DEVELOPMENT/ INDEPENDENT PRACTICE
Computer Test Bank Item Numbers			Worksheets/BLM's/Transp./Readings	Laboratories
Level 1	**Level 2**	**Level 3**		
11, 48	1, 12	13	**Reteaching: Blackline Master** 33 Basic Tissues of the Human Body **Transparency and Worksheet** 39 Basic Tissues of the Human Body	
2, 14, 15, 16, 17	18	19	**Review: Study Guide Exercise** A. Bones **Reteaching: Blackline Master** 34 Human Skeleton	
3, 20, 49, 50	21, 51		**Reteaching: Study Guide Exercise** B. Joints **Transparency and Worksheet** 40 Human Skeleton	
5, 26, 27, 28, 29	30, 53			
6, 54	31, 55	56	**Reteaching: Blackline Master** 34A Muscles of the Human Body **Enrichment: Study Guide Exercise** C. Critical Thinking: Muscle Contraction	
32, 33, 34, 35	7, 57	58, 59, 60		
36, 37, 61	38, 39	8		**Structured Lab Investigation:** 37A Bones and Muscles
40, 41, 62	9, 42	43; LAB 4, 22, 23, 24, 25, 52	**Reteaching: Transparency and Worksheet** 41 Muscles of the Human Body **Enrichment: Study Guide Exercise** D. Synthesis: Structure and Kinds of Muscles	**Lab Activity:** A Survey of Human Body Tissues, text page 625
44, 45, 63	10, 46	47	**Reteaching: Blackline Master** 35 Cross Section of Human Skin **Transparency and Worksheet** 42 Cross Section of Human Skin **Review: Study Guide Exercise** E. Anatomy and Function of Skin	

Chapter 38 Digestion and Nutrition

SECTION OBJECTIVES	Core	Average	Enriched	Text Section(s)	Checkpoint Item No.(s)	Chapt. Rev. Item No.(s)
UPPER ALIMENTARY CANAL **Text Sections 38-1 to 38-4**						
A *Compare* and *contrast* chemical digestion and mechanical digestion.	●	●	●	38-1	1, 5, 6	1, 19, 20
B *Explain* how structures in the mouth help prepare food for the rest of the digestive system.	●	●	●	38-2	2, 3, 6	1, 18
C *Describe* the structure and function of the esophagus.		●	●	38-3	4, 6	2, 21, 35
D *Identify* several functions of the stomach.	●	●	●	38-4	5, 6	3, 22
LOWER ALIMENTARY CANAL **Text Sections 38-5 to 38-8**						
E *List* the functions of the pancreas and the liver in digestion.		●	●	38-5	7, 8, 12	4, 5, 24, 32
F *Describe* the structure and function of the small intestine.				38-6, 38-7	9, 11	6, 7, 20, 23, 25
G *Explain* the function of the large intestine.				38-8	10	8, 26
NUTRITION **Text Sections 38-9 to 38-14**						
H *Describe* the unit which measures the energy content of food.	●	●	●	38-9	13	9, 28
I *Explain* the role of carbohydrates and fats in the diet.		●	●	38-10	14	10, 11, 29, 34
J *List* several functions of proteins in your diet.		●	●	38-11	14, 18	13, 31, 33, 34
K *List* some important vitamins and minerals in the diet and *identify* their function.		●	●	38-12	15, 18	14, 15, 34
L *Explain* what is meant by a balanced diet and why such a diet is important.	●	●	●	38-13	16, 18	16, 17, 30, 31, 33
M *Compare* two kinds of eating disorders.		●	●	38-14	17	12, 27

Vocabulary Review: Biology Crossword
CHAPTER 38 TEST

ASSESSMENT			CONTENT DEVELOPMENT/ GUIDED PRACTICE	PROCESS SKILL DEVELOPMENT/ INDEPENDENT PRACTICE
Computer Test Bank Item Numbers			Worksheets/BLM's/Transp./Readings	Laboratories
Level 1	Level 2	Level 3		
1, 11	43	12		
2, 13, 14, 44	15, 45	46, 47, 48		
3, 16	17	18		
4, 49	19, 50	51	**Reteaching: Study Guide Exercise** C. Mechanical Digestion	
5, 20, 21	22, 52			
6, 23, 24	25, 53		**Reteaching: Study Guide Exercise** D. Chemical Digestion	
26, 27, 28	29	30	**Reteaching: Study Guide Exercises** A. Organs of Digestion B. Functions of the Digestive System **Blackline Master** 36 Human Digestive System **Transparency and Worksheet** 43 Human Digestive System	**Structured Lab Investigation:** 38A Digestion and Nutrition
31, 32	7	54; LAB 41, 42, 64, 65		**Lab Activity:** Measuring Food Energy, text page 645
33, 34, 35	55, 56			**Inquiry Lab Investigation:** 38B Digestion of Fat
8, 36, 57	58		**Enrichment: Study Guide Exercise** E. Synthesis: Food Molecules	
59, 60, 61	9, 62		**Reteaching: Study Guide Exercise** G. Concept Mapping **Enrichment: Study Guide Exercise** F. Critical Thinking: Source and Function of Vitamins and Minerals	
10, 37	38	63		
39, 40				

Chapter 39 Respiration and Excretion

SECTION OBJECTIVES	Core	Average	Enriched	Text Section(s)	Checkpoint Item No.(s)	Chapt. Rev. Item No.(s)
RESPIRATION **Text Sections 39-1 to 39-5** A *Compare* and *contrast* external, internal, and cellular respiration.		●	●	39-1	1	1, 17, 20
B *Identify* the structures of the human respiratory system and *state* the function of each structure.	●	●	●	39-2	2, 3, 7	2, 3, 16, 18, 20, 28, 29, 30, 31, 35
C *Trace* the path of oxygen and carbon dioxide throughout the body.	●	●	●	39-3	4, 8, 9	5, 6, 17, 21, 35
D *Describe* how air enters and leaves the lungs.	●	●	●	39-4	5	7, 8, 19
E *Explain* the mechanism that controls breathing rate.		●	●	39-5	6	9, 23
EXCRETORY SYSTEM **Text Sections 39-6 to 39-10** F *Describe* the location and function of the kidneys.	●	●	●	39-6	10	10, 11, 22
G *Identify* the various parts of a nephron.		●	●	39-7	11	12, 13, 22, 34
H *Explain* the function of the nephron.		●	●	39-8	12, 15	14, 24, 27, 33, 34
I *State* how the kidneys serve a role in maintaining homeostasis of body fluids.		●	●	39-9	13	15, 26, 32
J *Explain* the methods used to treat kidney failure.			●	39-10	14	4, 25
Vocabulary Review: Biology Crossword **CHAPTER 39 TEST**						

ASSESSMENT			CONTENT DEVELOPMENT/ GUIDED PRACTICE	PROCESS SKILL DEVELOPMENT/ INDEPENDENT PRACTICE
Computer Test Bank Item Numbers			Worksheets/BLM's/Transp./Readings	Laboratories
Level 1	Level 2	Level 3		
1, 11, 12, 13	14, 37			
2, 16, 17	15, 18, 19		**Reteaching: Blackline Master** 37 Human Respiratory System	
3, 20	21, 65	22	**Enrichment: Study Guide Exercise** B. Critical Thinking: Gas Exchange	
23, 24, 38, 39	4	40	**Reteaching: Study Guide Exercise** A. Structure and Function of the Lungs **Transparency and Worksheet** 44 Human Respiratory System **Enrichment: Study Guide Exercise** C. Synthesis: Comparison of the Bird and the Human Respiratory Systems	**Structured Lab Investigation:** 39A Respiratory System
5, 25, 26, 41	42, 43		**Reteaching: Study Guide Exercise** D. Control of Breathing Rate	
6, 27, 44, 45	28, 46		**Reteaching: Study Guide Exercise** E. The Organs of Excretion	
7, 29, 47, 48	49	50; LAB 10, 33, 34, 35, 36, 63, 64	**Reteaching: Blackline Master** 38 Anatomy of a Human Kidney	**Lab Activity:** Lung and Kidney Structure, text page 661
8, 30, 51, 52	53	54		
31, 32, 55	9, 56	57, 58, 59, 60	**Reteaching: Transparency and Worksheet** 45 Anatomy of a Human Kidney	
61, 62				

Chapter 40 Circulation

SECTION OBJECTIVES	Core	Average	Enriched	Text Section(s)	Checkpoint Item No.(s)	Chapt. Rev. Item No.(s)
THE HEART AND BLOOD VESSELS **Text Sections 40-1 to 40-6** A *Identify* the anatomical features of the human heart.	●	●	●	40-1	1, 7	1, 16, 28
B *Describe* how the rate of the heart beat is controlled.		●	●	40-2	5	6, 19, 24
C *List* some causes of heart attacks.	●	●	●	40-3	6	15, 16, 30
D *Trace* the path of a single blood cell in a complete circuit throughout the circulatory system.		●	●	40-4	2, 8	2, 3, 17, 30
E *Compare* and *contrast* the structure and function of the three kinds of blood vessels.		●	●	40-5	3	3, 4, 22
F *Explain* the significance of blood pressure.	●	●	●	40-6	4	5, 18, 22
BLOOD AND LYMPH **Text Sections 40-7 to 40-11** G *Identify* several functions of blood plasma.		●	●	40-7	9	7, 26, 29
H *Describe* the function of red blood cells and *explain* blood types.		●	●	40-8	10, 11, 15, 16	8, 9, 20, 25, 27, 29
I *Contrast* the structure and function of white and red blood cells.		●	●	40-8, 40-9	12, 15	10, 11, 21, 25, 29
J *Give examples* of how the liver maintains homeostasis.			●	40-11	14	13, 14
K *List* the functions of the lymphatic system.		●	●	40-10	13	12, 23

Vocabulary Review: Biology Crossword
CHAPTER 40 TEST

ASSESSMENT			CONTENT DEVELOPMENT/ GUIDED PRACTICE	PROCESS SKILL DEVELOPMENT/ INDEPENDENT PRACTICE
Computer Test Bank Item Numbers			Worksheets/BLM's/Transp./Readings	Laboratories
Level 1	Level 2	Level 3		
11, 12, 13	1	14; LAB 5, 32, 33, 34, 35	**Reteaching: Blackline Master** 39 Anatomy of the Human Heart **Transparency and Worksheet** 46 Anatomy of the Human Heart **Review: Study Guide Exercise** A. The Heart	**Lab Activity:** The Structure of the Heart, text page 677
15, 16	17, 18	48		**Structured Lab Investigation:** 40A Circulation and Exercise
2, 19		20, 49, 50		
21, 22, 23	24, 25			
3, 26, 27	28		**Reteaching: Blackline Master** 40 Cross Section of Major Blood Vessels of the Human Circulatory System **Transparency and Worksheet** 47 Cross Sections of Major Vessels of the Human Circulatory System	
29, 30	31, 51	4	**Enrichment: Study Guide Exercise** B. Critical Thinking: Blood Pressure	
6, 36, 37	52, 53		**Review: Study Guide Exercise** C. Blood Clotting	
7, 38	39, 54	55	**Review: Study Guide Exercise** D. Blood Types **Enrichment: Study Guide Exercise** E. Synthesis: Blood Type Inheritance	
8, 40, 41	42, 56			
9, 43, 44, 45	57	58, 59		**Enrichment:** BIOSOLVE Software: Toxicology, Short and Long Investigations
10, 46, 47	60, 61		**Review: Study Guide Exercise** F. Concept Mapping	

SECTION OBJECTIVES	Core	Average	Enriched	Text Section(s)	Checkpoint Item No.(s)	Chapt. Rev. Item No.(s)
INFECTIOUS DISEASE **Text Sections 41-1 to 41-2** A *Explain* Robert Koch's contribution to bacteriology.		●	●	41-1	1, 5	1, 15
B *Explain* how bacteria and viruses cause disease when they enter the human body.	●	●	●	41-1	2, 3, 6	2, 3, 15, 16, 21
C *List* several ways that disease can be transmitted from one person to another.	●	●	●	41-2	4, 7	4, 17, 18, 19, 30, 34
THE BODY'S DEFENSES **Text Sections 41-3 to 41-7** D *Identify* your body's primary barriers to invasion by pathogens.	●	●	●	41-3	8, 9, 15	5
E *Describe* the major parts of the human immune system.		●	●	41-4	10	6, 20
F *Explain* the role of antibodies in fighting disease organisms.		●	●	41-5	11	22, 31, 32
G *State* how the various leucocytes of the immune system play a role in defending against disease and establishing immunity.		●	●	41-6	12, 14	7, 8, 22, 25, 26, 31, 32
H *Describe* the effects of the AIDS virus on the immune system.	●	●	●	41-7	13	9, 27, 34
TREATING DISEASE **Text Sections 41-8 to 41-11** I *Explain* how vaccines function.		●	●	41-8	16, 18, 19	23, 26, 32
J *Describe* how chemicals can sometimes help treat disease.		●	●	41-9	17, 19	10, 24, 28, 29, 33
K *Describe* two types of immune system malfunctions.			●	41-10		11
L *List* reasons why drugs might be used to alter the activities of the immune system.			●	41-11	20	12, 31
M *Describe* the potential uses of lymphokines and monoclonal antibodies.			●	41-11	21, 22	13, 14

Vocabulary Review: Biology Crossword
CHAPTER 41 TEST

ASSESSMENT			CONTENT DEVELOPMENT/ GUIDED PRACTICE	PROCESS SKILL DEVELOPMENT/ INDEPENDENT PRACTICE
Computer Test Bank Item Numbers			Worksheets/BLM's/Transp./Readings	Laboratories
Level 1	**Level 2**	**Level 3**		
1, 40	41			
11, 12	2	42	**Enrichment: Cutting Edge** New Diseases, text pages 696–697	
3, 13	14	43; LAB 36, 37, 38, 39, 63	**Reteaching: Study Guide Exercise** A. How Infectious Diseases Are Transmitted	**Lab Activity:** Microorganisms in the Environment, text page 695 **Enrichment: BIOSOLVE Software:** Infectious Disease, Short Investigation
15, 16, 17	4, 18			
19, 20, 44	5, 21		**Enrichment: Issues in Bioethics** Case Study 1, text page 766	
6, 22, 23, 45	46	24		
47, 48	7, 49, 50	57	**Reteaching: Study Guide Exercises** B. The Body's Defenses C. The Immune System D. Active and Passive Immunity **Transparency and Worksheet** 48 Immune System Process	**Enrichment:** BIOSOLVE Software: Infectious Disease, Long Investigation
25, 51	8	52	**Enrichment: Study Guide Exercise** E. Synthesis: AIDS Virus	
53, 54	9	26		
27, 28	55	56, 58		**Structured Lab Investigation:** 41A Testing Bactericides
10, 29, 59, 60	30			
31, 32	61			
33, 34, 62	35		**Enrichment: Study Guide Exercise** F. Critical Thinking: Genetic Engineering to Produce a Vaccine	

SECTION OBJECTIVES	Core	Average	Enriched	Text Section(s)	Checkpoint Item No.(s)	Chapt. Rev. Item No.(s)
TRANSMISSION OF INFORMATION **Text Sections 42-1 to 42-2** A *Distinguish* between different types of neurons.	●	●	●	42-1	1	1
B *Name* the parts of a neuron.	●	●	●	42-1	2	18
C *Describe* the role of the synapse.		●	●	42-1	3	2, 21
D *Explain* how a nerve impulse is transmitted.		●	●	42-2	4	16, 17, 20
E *Relate* the role of neurotransmitters to muscle function.			●	42-2	5	8
CENTRAL AND PERIPHERAL NERVOUS SYSTEMS **Text Sections 42-3 to 42-7** F *Describe* the structure and function of the cerebrum.		●	●	42-4	6	3, 20
G *Name* several brain structures and their functions.	●	●	●	42-3, 42-5	7	4, 19, 20
H *State* two functions of the spinal cord.		●	●	42-6	8	14, 15
I *Distinguish* the parts of the peripheral nervous system from each other.		●	●	42-7	9	5, 9
J *Identify* some nervous system disorders.			●	42-6	10	13

ASSESSMENT			CONTENT DEVELOPMENT/ GUIDED PRACTICE	PROCESS SKILL DEVELOPMENT/ INDEPENDENT PRACTICE
Computer Test Bank Item Numbers			Worksheets/BLM's/Transp./Readings	Laboratories
Level 1	**Level 2**	**Level 3**		
1, 11, 13	12	43		
14, 44, 45	46			
2, 47	48	15		
16, 49	17	3, 50, 51	**Reteaching: Blackline Master** 41 Structure and Function of a Human Neuron **Transparency and Worksheet** 49 Structure and Function of a Human Neuron **Review: Study Guide Exercise** A. Neurons and Nerves **Enrichment: Study Guide Exercise** B. Synthesis: Active Transport in Nerve Impulses	
4, 18	52			
5, 19	20, 21		**Review: Study Guide Exercise** D. Functions of the Areas of the Cerebrum	
22, 23	24, 25		**Review: Study Guide Exercise** C. The Brain	
26, 27	53		**Reteaching: Blackline Master** 42 The Human Nervous System **Transparency and Worksheet** 50 Human Nervous System **Review: Study Guide Exercise** E. Concept Mapping	
6, 28, 29	54	55	**Enrichment: Study Guide Exercise** F. Critical Thinking: Functions of the Autonomic Nervous System	**Structured Lab Investigation:** 42A Reflex Responses and Receptors
30	56, 57	58		

SECTION OBJECTIVES	Core	Average	Enriched	Text Section(s)	Checkpoint Item No.(s)	Chapt. Rev. Item No.(s)
THE SENSES **Text Sections 42-8 to 42-12** K *Name* the types of sense receptors located in the skin.	●	●	●	42-8	11	11
L *Explain* why taste and smell are called "chemical senses."		●	●	42-9, 42-10	12	6, 22
M *Relate* the structure of the ear to the sense of hearing.		●	●	42-11	13	10
N *Describe* the structure of the eye.		●	●	42-12	14	7, 12, 20
Vocabulary Review: Biology Crossword **CHAPTER 42 TEST**						

ASSESSMENT			CONTENT DEVELOPMENT/ GUIDED PRACTICE	PROCESS SKILL DEVELOPMENT/ INDEPENDENT PRACTICE
Computer Test Bank Item Numbers			Worksheets/BLM's/Transp./Readings	Laboratories
Level 1	Level 2	Level 3		
7, 31, 32	33	LAB 10, 40, 41, 42		**Lab Activity:** Skin Sensitivity to Touch, text page 715
8, 59	34, 60			
35, 36, 37	61		**Reteaching: Study Guide Exercise** G. Hearing and Balance **Blackline Master** 43 Anatomy of a Human Ear **Transparency and Worksheet** 51 Anatomy of a Human Ear	
9, 38, 39	62		**Reteaching: Blackline Master** 44 Anatomy of a Human Eye **Transparency and Worksheet** 52 Anatomy of a Human Eye	

SECTION OBJECTIVES	Core	Average	Enriched	Text Section(s)	Checkpoint Item No.(s)	Chapt. Rev. Item No.(s)
A DELICATE BALANCE **Text Sections 43-1 to 43-3**						
A *State* how hormones contribute to maintaining homeostasis.	●	●	●	Introduction	1	19
B *Distinguish* between the ways the nervous and endocrine systems coordinate activities in the body.			●	43-1	2	11, 29
C *Describe* the significance of target cells and receptors.		●	●	43-3	3, 7	13, 20, 35
D *Compare* the actions of two types of hormones on their target cells.		●	●	43-3	4, 6, 7	13, 14, 20, 35
E *Name* several hormones and state their sources and functions.		●	●	43-2	1, 5	1–8, 9, 17, 21, 25, 27
ENDOCRINE GLANDS AT WORK **Text Sections 43-4 to 43-9**						
F *Describe* the relationship between the hypothalamus and pituitary.		●	●	43-4	10, 11, 16	9, 23, 24, 29, 31
G *State* the role of hypothalmic releasing factors.		●	●	43-4	9, 17	9, 12, 25, 28
H *Explain* how negative feedback works.	●	●	●	43-5	12	16, 23, 26, 34
I *Name* the functions regulated by the sex hormones.		●	●	43-6	13	10, 22
J *Describe* how insulin and glucagon work as regulators of the same body condition.		●	●	43-7	14	15, 30, 33, 35
K *Identify* the endocrine roles of other body structures.			●	43-8	15	1–8, 26
L *List* some recent developments in the field of endocrinology.			●	43-9	18	18, 32

Vocabulary Review: Biology Crossword
CHAPTER 43 TEST

ASSESSMENT			CONTENT DEVELOPMENT/ GUIDED PRACTICE	PROCESS SKILL DEVELOPMENT/ INDEPENDENT PRACTICE
Computer Test Bank Item Numbers			Worksheets/BLM's/Transp./Readings	Laboratories
Level 1	**Level 2**	**Level 3**		
1, 11, 42	43			
2, 12		44	**Enrichment: Study Guide Exercise** A. Synthesis: Comparing the Endocrine System and Nervous System	
3, 13, 45	14, 15			
16	17, 18, 19	46, 47, 48, 49		
20, 21	4, 22	50		**Structured Lab Investigation:** 43A Adrenaline and Daphnia
5, 23, 24, 25	26			
6, 51	27	52		
28, 29, 53	7	54; LAB 39, 40, 41, 64		**Lab Activity:** Hormones and Feedback Systems, text page 731
8, 30, 55	56	31	**Enrichment: Study Guide Exercise** C. Critical Thinking: Control Mechanisms	
32	33, 57, 58	59	**Review: Study Guide Exercise** B. Hormones in Balance	**Enrichment:** BIOSOLVE Software, Internal Medicine, Short and Long Investigations
9, 34, 35	60, 61			
10, 36, 37, 62	38, 63			

Chapter 44 Substance Abuse

SECTION OBJECTIVES	Core	Average	Enriched	Text Section(s)	Checkpoint Item No.(s)	Chapt. Rev. Item No.(s)
DRUGS AND ABUSE **Text Sections 44-1 to 44-3** A *List* the effects of several drugs that are abused.	●	●	●	44-2	1	3, 5, 10, 13, 19, 20, 23, 25
B *Distinguish* between psychological and physical dependence.	●	●	●	44-1	2	9, 18, 25
C *Distinguish* among stimulants, depressants, natural, and synthetic drugs.		●	●	44-2	4	7, 14, 21
D *Explain* how the function of endorphins is tied to the action of narcotics.		●	●	44-3	3, 5	17
ALCOHOL AND TOBACCO **Text Sections 44-4 to 44-8** E *Describe* the immediate action of alcohol on the body.	●	●	●	44-4	6, 7	8, 28, 30
F *Explain* why driving under the influence of alcohol is illegal.	●	●	●	44-4	6	11
G *Describe* the long-term effects of alcohol on the body.		●	●	44-5	6, 8, 9, 10	12, 26, 29
H *Describe* the hazards and diseases associated with smoking, tobacco, and smoke.	●	●	●	44-6, 44-7	11, 12, 13, 14	1, 2, 4, 6, 15, 16, 22, 24
I *List* practices that reflect a responsible use of drugs.	●	●	●	44-8	15	27, 29

Vocabulary Review: Biology Crossword
CHAPTER 44 TEST

ASSESSMENT			CONTENT DEVELOPMENT/ GUIDED PRACTICE	PROCESS SKILL DEVELOPMENT/ INDEPENDENT PRACTICE
Computer Test Bank Item Numbers			Worksheets/BLM's/Transp./Readings	Laboratories
Level 1	**Level 2**	**Level 3**		
1, 11, 12, 42	13, 43	44		
2, 14, 45	46	15	**Enrichment: Study Guide Exercise** C. Synthesis: Narcotics and the Nervous System	
16, 47, 48	3, 17, 18, 19			
20, 21, 22	23, 49		**Review: Study Guide Exercise** A. Dependence on Drugs	
4, 24, 25, 50, 51	26	52, 53; LAB 10, 36, 37, 38, 39, 40, 41		**Inquiry Lab Investigation:** 44A Alcohol and Seed Germination **Lab Activity:** Effect of Drugs on the Heart Rate, text page 745
5, 27, 54	28, 55			
6, 29, 30, 3	56	57		
7, 32, 33, 58	59, 60	34	**Enrichment: Study Guide Exercise** B. Critical Thinking: Effects of Tobacco **Biology Matters** 10 The Tobacco Controversy: A Question of Rights	
8, 35	9, 61	62	**Enrichment: *Biology Matters*** 9 Drug Testing: A Constitutional Issue	

SECTION OBJECTIVES	Core	Average	Enriched	Text Section(s)	Checkpoint Item No.(s)	Chapt. Rev. Item No.(s)
THE STRUCTURES OF REPRODUCTION **Text Sections 45-1 to 45-3** A *List* the parts of the male and female reproductive systems and their functions.	●	●	●	45-1, 45-2	1, 4	1, 19, 23
B *Compare* the production of sperm and eggs.		●	●	45-1, 45-2	2, 5	1, 2, 3, 4, 6, 20, 24
C *Trace* the path of sperm and eggs from their points of origin to the point at which they meet.	●	●	●	45-1, 45-2	3	2, 4, 11, 23, 27, 30, 31
D *Relate* the levels of hormones to changes in the ovary and uterine lining during the menstrual cycle.		●	●	45-3	6	6, 7, 9, 10, 22, 25, 32, 33
THE PROCESS OF REPRODUCTION **Text Sections 45-4 to 45-9** E *Identify* the fertile period in the menstrual cycle.	●	●	●	45-4	8	8, 10
F *Describe* the process of fertilization.		●	●	45-4	11	11, 31, 35, 36
G *List* the stages that occur between zygote and fetus.		●	●	45-5, 45-6	7	12, 15, 16, 18
H *State* the origins and function of the embryonic membranes.			●	45-5, 45-6	9	12, 13, 16, 34
I *Contrast* the development of identical and fraternal twins.		●	●	45-9	10	14, 21, 29

ASSESSMENT Computer Test Bank Item Numbers			CONTENT DEVELOPMENT/ GUIDED PRACTICE Worksheets/BLM's/Transp./Readings	PROCESS SKILL DEVELOPMENT/ INDEPENDENT PRACTICE Laboratories
Level 1	Level 2	Level 3		
1, 11, 12, 49	50, 51		**Reteaching: Blackline Masters** 44A Reproductive System of a Human Male 44C Reproductive System of a Human Female **Transparencies and Worksheets** 53 Reproductive System of a Human Male 54 Reproductive System of a Human Female **Review: Study Guide Exercise** A. Anatomy of the Male and Female Reproductive Systems	
2, 13, 14, 15	16, 52		**Reteaching: Blackline Master** 44B Formation of Human Eggs and Sperm	
17, 53, 72	3, 18			
19, 20, 54	21, 22	23, 55, 56	**Reteaching: Transparency and Worksheet** 55 The Human Menstrual Cycle	
24, 25, 26	4, 57	58		
5, 27, 28, 29	30	59		
6, 31, 32	33, 34	60; LAB 10, 46, 47, 48, 71	**Review: Study Guide Exercise** B. Fertilization and Early Embryonic Development **Enrichment: Study Guide Exercises** C. Critical Thinking: Placental Hormone D. Synthesis: Gastrulation	**Structured Lab Investigation:** 45A Chick Embryo Development **Lab Activity:** The Development of a Fertilized Egg
35, 61, 62	63, 64	65	**Reteaching: Blackline Master** 45 Structure of a Human Embryo **Transparency and Worksheet** 56 Structure of a Human Embryo	
7, 36, 37, 66	38	39		

SECTION OBJECTIVES	Core	Average	Enriched	Text Section(s)	Checkpoint Item No.(s)	Chapt. Rev. Item No.(s)
J *Name* several factors that can harm an embryo.	●	●	●	45-7	12	17, 28
K *Describe* the changes that occur in the mother and baby immediately before, during, and after birth.		●	●	45-8	13	25, 26

Vocabulary Review: Biology Crossword
CHAPTER 45 TEST
Unit 7 Concept Review:
Concept Mapping Exercise
Unit 7 Review, text page 767

ASSESSMENT			CONTENT DEVELOPMENT/ GUIDED PRACTICE	PROCESS SKILL DEVELOPMENT/ INDEPENDENT PRACTICE
Computer Test Bank Item Numbers			Worksheets/BLM's/Transp./Readings	Laboratories
Level 1	Level 2	Level 3		
8, 40, 41, 42	67, 68		**Enrichment: Issues in Bioethics** Case Study 2, text page 766	
9, 43, 44, 69	45	70		

SECTION OBJECTIVES	Core	Average	Enriched	Text Section(s)	Checkpoint Item No.(s)	Chapt. Rev. Item No.(s)
INSTINCT AND LEARNING						
Text Sections 46-1 to 46-4						
A *Explain* how natural selection acts on behavior.	●	●	●	46-1	1, 7	18, 20
B *Give examples* of innate behavior.	●	●	●	46-2	2, 5	1, 4, 7, 16, 17
C *Distinguish* between innate and learned behavior.	●	●	●	46-3	3	15, 23
D *State* the advantages of innate and learned behavior.		●	●	46-3	6	2, 3, 23
E *Name* several types of learning and *give examples* of each.		●	●	46-4	4	6, 19, 25
PATTERNS OF BEHAVIOR						
Text Sections 46-5 to 46-9						
F *Name* three types of orientation behavior.		●	●	46-5	8	5, 14, 16, 17
G *State* the adaptive significance of courtship.			●	46-6	9	8, 16, 22, 24
H *Explain* the functions of territoriality and aggression.		●	●	46-7	11	11, 12, 18, 22
I *List* the advantages of social behavior.		●	●	46-8	12	9, 13, 21, 24
J *Give examples* of communication among animals.		●	●	46-9	10	10

Vocabulary Review: Biology Crossword
CHAPTER 46 TEST

ASSESSMENT			CONTENT DEVELOPMENT/ GUIDED PRACTICE	PROCESS SKILL DEVELOPMENT/ INDEPENDENT PRACTICE
Computer Test Bank Item Numbers			Worksheets/BLM's/Transp./Readings	Laboratories
Level 1	Level 2	Level 3		
1, 11, 37	38	39		
2, 12	13, 40	41	**Review: Study Guide Exercise** A. Forms of Behavior	
3, 42, 43	44, 45			
4, 14, 46	15, 47, 48			
5, 16, 49	17	50, 51; LAB 18, 19, 20, 21, 22, 23		**Structured Lab Investigation:** 46A Human Behavior **Lab Activity:** Learning by Trial-and-Error, text page 779
6, 24, 25	52, 53	54	**Enrichment: Study Guide Exercise** C. Critical Thinking: Migratory Memory	
26, 27, 55	7, 56	57	**Enrichment: Study Guide Exercise** B. Synthesis: Hormones and Behavior	
28, 29, 30, 58	8	59		
9, 31, 32, 33, 34	60			
10, 35, 36, 61	62		**Review: Study Guide Exercise** D. Selective Advantage of Patterns of Behavior	

SECTION OBJECTIVES	Core	Average	Enriched	Text Section(s)	Checkpoint Item No.(s)	Chapt. Rev. Item No.(s)
BIOMES ON LAND **Text Sections 47-1 to 47-10** A *Describe* how biomes are determined by climate.		●	●	47-2	1	1, 28
B *Identify* the major terrestrial biomes and *describe* the main characteristics of each.	●	●	●	47-1, 47-3–47-9	2, 3, 6	3, 4, 8, 11–16, 17, 18, 20, 21, 25, 27
C *Give examples* of plant and animal adaptations to climate.		●	●	47-3–47-9	4	5, 6, 19, 25
D *Compare* the effects of latitude and altitude on the sequence of biomes.		●	●	47-10	5	7, 26
AQUATIC BIOMES **Text Sections 47-11 to 47-13** E *Identify* the abiotic factors that influence the distribution of aquatic organisms.		●	●	47-11	8, 10	2, 9, 22, 23
F *Describe* the major life zones of the ocean and *give* the characteristics of each.		●	●	47-11	7	22, 23, 27
G *Distinguish* between standing water and running water biomes.		●	●	47-12	8, 11	10, 24
H *Explain* how an estuary differs from other aquatic biomes.		●	●	47-13	9	

Vocabulary Review: Biology Crossword
CHAPTER 47 TEST

ASSESSMENT			CONTENT DEVELOPMENT/ GUIDED PRACTICE	PROCESS SKILL DEVELOPMENT/ INDEPENDENT PRACTICE
Computer Test Bank Item Numbers			Worksheets/BLM's/Transp./Readings	Laboratories
Level 1	Level 2	Level 3		
1, 11, 12	2, 38, 39	40		
3, 13, 14, 41	4, 42	43	**Reteaching: Blackline Master** 46 The Six World Biomes **Review: Study Guide Exercise** C. Mapping the World's Biomes **Enrichment: Biology Matters** 11 Going, Going, Gone: What Is Happening to the Tropical Rain Forests?	
5, 15, 44	16, 45, 46	LAB 10, 34, 35, 36, 37, 60		**Structured Lab Investigation:** Plant Adaptations to Land Biomes **Lab Activity:** Soil Properties and Plant Growth
17, 18, 19, 20, 61	21, 47	48		
6, 22, 49	50	51		
7, 23, 24, 25, 52	26, 27			**Structured Lab Investigation:** 47B Marine Environments
8, 28, 29, 30, 31	53, 54	55	**Enrichment: Study Guide Exercise** A. Synthesis: Freshwater Biomes	
9, 56	32, 33	57, 58, 59	**Enrichment: Study Guide Exercise** B. Critical Thinking: Estuaries	

SECTION OBJECTIVES	Core	Average	Enriched	Text Section(s)	Checkpoint Item No.(s)	Chapt. Rev. Item No.(s)
LIVING COMMUNITIES **Text Sections 48-1 to 48-5**						
A *Describe* the characteristics of an ecosystem.	●	●	●	48-1	1, 7	4
B *Identify* the roles of organisms in an ecosystem.	●	●	●	48-2	2	14, 17
C *Diagram* the feeding levels in food chains and food webs.		●	●	48-3	3, 6	1, 2, 13, 15, 16, 21, 23, 25, 27
D *Explain* how a pyramid can be used to represent energy flow in a food web.		●	●	48-4	4	5, 16, 18, 26, 29
E *Give examples* of symbiosis.	●	●	●	48-5	5	6, 9, 19
CHANGES IN COMMUNITIES **Text Sections 48-6 to 48-7** F *Give examples* of the changes that occur during succession.		●	●	48-6	8	8
G *Distinguish* between primary and secondary succession.		●	●	48-6, 48-7	9	11
H *Contrast* a pioneer community with a climax community.		●	●	48-6	10, 11	12
CYCLES IN THE BIOSPHERE **Text Sections 48-8 to 48-11** I *Describe* how the supply of fresh water in the biosphere is maintained.	●	●	●	48-8	12	7, 24
J *Explain* how carbon and oxygen are recycled between organisms and the atmosphere.		●	●	48-9, 48-11	13, 14, 16	2, 18, 20, 22, 28
K *Give examples* of the forms of nitrogen produced during the nitrogen cycle.			●	48-10	15	3, 10, 30
Vocabulary Review: Biology Crossword **CHAPTER 48 TEST**						

ASSESSMENT			CONTENT DEVELOPMENT/ GUIDED PRACTICE	PROCESS SKILL DEVELOPMENT/ INDEPENDENT PRACTICE
Computer Test Bank Item Numbers			Worksheets/BLM's/Transp./Readings	Laboratories
Level 1	Level 2	Level 3		
11, 12, 13	1, 40			
2, 14, 15	41	42		
3, 16, 43	44, 45	46, 47, 48	**Reteaching: Transparency and Worksheet** 57 Food Web **Review: Study Guide Exercise** A. Energy Flow in Ecosystems	**Structured Lab Investigation:** 48A Pond Ecosystem
4, 17, 18	49	50	**Enrichment: Study Guide Exercise** B. Critical Thinking: Energy Pyramids	
5, 19	20, 51	21		
22	52, 53	6		
23, 24, 54	7, 25			
8, 55	26, 56		**Enrichment: Study Guide Exercise** C. Synthesis: Succession in a Community	
27, 28, 29	30	31	**Reteaching: Transparency and Worksheet** 58 Water Cycle	
32, 33, 57	34, 58		**Reteaching: Transparency and Worksheet** 59 Carbon Cycle **Review: Study Guide Exercise** D. Carbon Cycle	
9, 35, 36	37, 59	LAB 10, 38, 39, 60, 61	**Reteaching: Transparency and Worksheet** 60 Nitrogen Cycle	**Lab Activity:** Examination of Nitrogen-Fixing Bacteria, text page 813

SECTION OBJECTIVES	Core	Average	Enriched	Text Section(s)	Checkpoint Item No.(s)	Chapt. Rev. Item No.(s)
POPULATION GROWTH PATTERNS						
Text Sections 49-1 to 49-3						
A *Explain* why populations do not reach their biotic potential.		●	●	49-1	1, 4	1, 13
B *Discuss* the relationship between growth rate and carrying capacity.			●	49-2	2	2, 14, 15, 16, 21, 23, 24
C *List* several factors that affect population size.	●	●	●	49-3	3	3, 4, 19, 24
ENVIRONMENTAL RESISTANCE						
Text Sections 49-4 to 49-5						
D *Name* several density-independent factors that limit population growth.		●	●	49-4	5	5
E *Give examples* of factors that are density-dependent.		●	●	49-5	6	7, 8, 12
F *Explain* how prey-predator relationships help to regulate population growth.		●	●	49-5	8	6, 18, 22
G *Distinguish* between interspecific and intraspecific competition.		●	●	49-5	7	17
THE HUMAN POPULATION						
Text Sections 49-6 to 49-7						
H *Give* several reasons for the high growth rate of the human population.	●	●	●	49-6	9, 11	19, 20
I *Contrast* the growth rates of populations that have undergone demographic transition with those of populations that have not.			●	49-6	10, 12	9, 10
J *Discuss* the importance of uncontrolled population growth in terms of carrying capacity.		●	●	49-7	13	11
Vocabulary Review: Biology Crossword **CHAPTER 49 TEST**						

ASSESSMENT			CONTENT DEVELOPMENT/ GUIDED PRACTICE	PROCESS SKILL DEVELOPMENT/ INDEPENDENT PRACTICE
Computer Test Bank Item Numbers			Worksheets/BLM's/Transp./Readings	Laboratories
Level 1	Level 2	Level 3		
11, 12, 36, 37	1, 38			
13, 39	40, 41	42	**Review: Study Guide Exercise** A. Growth of Populations **Enrichment: Study Guide Exercise** B. Critical Thinking: Population Size	
2, 14, 43	15	44, 45, 46, 47		
4, 19, 50	20, 51			
5, 21, 22, 52	53, 54	LAB 3, 16, 17, 18, 48, 49	**Enrichment: Study Guide Exercise** C. Synthesis: Competition	**Structured Lab Investigation:** 49A Population Crowding **Lab Activity:** Effect of Different Reproductive Patterns on Population Size, text page 825
6, 23	24	55		
25, 26, 56	7, 27, 28	29		
8, 30, 57	58	31		
9, 32, 59, 60	33, 61			
10, 34, 35, 62	63		**Review: Study Guide Exercise** D. World Population Growth	

SECTION OBJECTIVES	Core	Average	Enriched	Text Section(s)	Checkpoint Item No.(s)	Chapt. Rev. Item No.(s)
NATURAL RESOURCES **Text Sections 50-1 to 50-4** A *Identify* important natural resources.	●	●	●	50-1, 50-2, 50-3, 50-4	1	2, 18
B *Distinguish* between renewable and nonrenewable resources.	●	●	●	Introduction	2, 5	2, 4, 17, 21
C *Explain* how human activities endanger natural resources.	●	●	●	50-1, 50-2, 50-3, 50-4	3	5, 19, 25, 28
D *Give examples* of methods to preserve natural resources.	●	●	●	50-1, 50-2, 50-3, 50-4	4	3, 11–15, 20, 21, 22, 23, 25
ENERGY RESOURCES **Text Sections 50-5 to 50-9** E *Identify* different types of energy resources.		●	●	50-5, 50-6, 50-7, 50-8	6	6, 7, 17, 27
F *Distinguish* between renewable and nonrenewable energy resources.		●	●	Introduction	7, 9	6
G *Describe* ways to conserve energy.	●	●	●	50-9	8	11–15, 20, 21, 23, 26
POLLUTION **Text Sections 50-10 to 50-12** H *Explain* how population size and lifestyle affect pollution.		●	●	Introduction, 50-10, 50-11, 50-12	10	16, 26
I *List* several types of pollution and their causes.		●	●	50-10, 50-11, 50-12	11	1, 8, 25
J *Give examples* of the hazards of pollution.	●	●	●	50-10, 50-11, 50-12	12, 13	9, 10, 24
K *Describe* methods used to reduce pollution.	●	●	●	50-10, 50-11, 50-12	14, 15	11–15, 21, 23, 25, 26

Vocabulary Review: Biology Crossword
CHAPTER 50 TEST
Unit 8 Concept Review: Concept Mapping Exercise
Unit 8 Review, text page 845

ASSESSMENT			CONTENT DEVELOPMENT/ GUIDED PRACTICE	PROCESS SKILL DEVELOPMENT/ INDEPENDENT PRACTICE
Computer Test Bank Item Numbers			Worksheets/BLM's/Transp./Readings	Laboratories
Level 1	Level 2	Level 3		
11, 33, 34	1, 35			
12, 36	2			
3, 37	38, 39	13	**Enrichment: Study Guide Exercise** B. Critical Thinking: Nutrients in a Forest	**Inquiry Lab Investigation:** 50A Pollutants
14, 15, 16, 40	4		**Enrichment: Study Guide Exercise** A. Synthesis: Soil Erosion **Issues in Bioethics** Case Study 2, text page 844	
5, 22, 41, 42	43	44		
45	46, 47	23	**Reteaching: Study Guide Exercise** D. Concept Mapping **Review: Study Guide Exercise** C. Alternative Energy Sources	
6, 48	24, 49	25	**Reteaching: Study Guide Exercise** E. Energy Conservation	
7, 50	26, 51	52		
8, 27, 53	54, 55	56; LAB 17, 18, 19, 20, 21	**Review: Study Guide Exercise** F. Pollution	**Lab Activity:** Effects of Acid Rain, text page 841
28, 29, 30	9, 31, 57	58, 59	**Enrichment: Issues in Bioethics** Case Study 1, text page 844	
32, 60	10, 61	62	**Enrichment: Biology Matters** 12 Water Crisis on Tap	